Applying Social Media Technologies in Healthcare Environments

Editor
Christina Beach Thielst, MHA, FACHE

HIMSS Mission

To globally lead endeavors optimizing health engagements and care outcomes through information technology.

© 2014 by Healthcare Information and Management Systems Society (HIMSS).

Printed in the U.S.A. 5 4 3 2 1

Requests for permission to make copies of any part of this work should be sent to:
Permissions Editor
HIMSS
33 W. Monroe St., Suite 1700
Chicago, IL 60603-5616
nancy.vitucci@himssmedia.com

ISBN: 978-1-938904-67-7

For more information about HIMSS, please visit www.himss.org.

About the Editor

Christina Beach Thielst, MHA, FACHE is a health administration and strategy consultant. A former hospital administrator, she helps clients improve their performance and create innovative strategies to transform the care delivery system. She views health information technology through an operations and risk management lens and is recognized as a thought leader in the field.

In 2005, she launched her blog, Christina's Considerations, and soon after began monitoring social media use by hospitals and other healthcare organizations. In 2013 her blog was selected as an addition to the National Library of Medicine's collection and archive of blogs on medicine and public health. She is the author of *Social Media in Healthcare: Connect Communicate Collaborate, 2nd edition*, an overview of social tools for healthcare leaders.

Christina's first book for HIMSS, *Guide to Establishing a Regional Health Information Exchange*, was published in 2007 and she was recognized with the Spirit of HIMSS award in April of that year.

Christina received a BS in social science/management from Louisiana State University and a Master's of Health Administration from Tulane University School of Public Health and Tropical Medicine. She is a Fellow of the American College of Healthcare Executives and a member of HIMSS and the American Telemedicine Association.

About the Contributors

Melissa E. Abraham, PhD, MSc is a Chairperson of the Partners HealthCare Human Research Committee and on the faculty at Harvard Medical School and the Mongan Institute for Health Policy, Massachusetts General Hospital. Dr. Abraham reviews research and provides guidance to the research community about ethical review of health-related studies involving social and behavioral components. Dr. Abraham received a PhD in clinical psychology from Northwestern University Medical School, an MSc in epidemiology from the Harvard School of Public Health, and completed a fellowship in medical ethics at Harvard Medical School.

Brian Ahier is a national expert on health information technology with a focus on health data exchange. He is President of Advanced Health Information Exchange Resources, LLC, which has provided consulting services to a variety of industry clients as well as the Office of the National Coordinator at HHS. Brian is a member of the Consumer Technology Workgroup of the HIT Standards Committee. Brian is a founding board member of DirectTrust, and also serves on the board of HIMSS Oregon and Q-Life, an intergovernmental agency providing broadband capacity to the region. Brian helped found Gorge Health Connect, Inc. (GHC), a health information exchange organization that implemented one of the first Direct Project pilots. Brian worked at Mid-Columbia Medical Center for eleven years, most recently as Health IT Evangelist. Brian helped develop the Oregon strategic and operational plans for implementing state-level HIE under the State Health Information Exchange Cooperative Agreement. He was appointed by the State of Oregon Health Information Technology Oversight Council (HITOC) as Chairperson of the Technology Workgroup responsible for developing a framework and providing input for technology goals. Brian has worked on a number of workgroups and committees within the Standards and Interoperability Framework and continues to work on the Direct Project.

Amanda Biegler Wall, MSHI leads a team of digital strategists at Children's Medical Center Dallas, a HIMSS Stage 7, Most Wired, and Enterprise HIMSS Davies Award of Excellence winning healthcare system. Focusing on digital solutions that span the continuum of care, Amanda has overseen several website and portal builds, integrating the care a patient receives inside the four walls of the hospital with the support and resources available to them at home. Amanda enjoys working in the digital healthcare world because the technology is always evolving, and the benefit to patients and their families is so apparent. She completed her undergraduate work in marketing and arts at Baylor University and received her Master's degree in Healthcare Informatics from Northwestern University.

Kashif Firozvi, MD completed his undergraduate studies at Johns Hopkins University and received his medical degree at Georgetown University School of Medicine. He remained there to complete his residency in internal medicine. Dr. Firozvi continued on to complete a fellowship in hematology and oncology at Georgetown's Lombardi Cancer Center. While at Lombardi, he completed a fellowship in developmental therapeutics, during which he was actively involved in clinical research in drug development. He is aware of cutting-edge and investigative cancer therapies and provides compassionate care tailored to each patient. He also serves as Clinical Assistant Professor of Medicine at Georgetown University School of Medicine.

David Gelber, MD, FACS graduated from Johns Hopkins University in 1980 and graduated in 1984 from the University of Rochester School of Medicine. He completed his residency at Baylor University Medical Center in Dallas, Texas, followed by three years as attending surgeon at Nassau County Medical Center in Long Island, New York. Gelber has since joined Coastal Surgical Group in Houston, Texas. Gelber has been a surgeon for more than 20 years, but over the last few years he began to pursue his passion for writing. He has written several novels, as well as two books about surgery: *Behind the Mask and Under the Drapes.* Dr. Gelber is married with three children, four dogs and a variety of birds. His interests include horse racing, mechanical Swiss watches and, of course, writing.

Timothy M. Hale, PhD is a Research Fellow at the Center for Connected Health and Harvard Medical School. He received his PhD in medical sociology from the University of Alabama, Birmingham. His research examines how new information and communication technologies (ICTs) are transforming existing models of healthcare and the emergence of digital health lifestyles. His work has been published in *American Behavioral Scientist, Information, Communication & Society, Journal of Health Communication*, and *Social Science Quarterly*.

David Harlow, JD, MPH is Principal of The Harlow Group LLC, a healthcare law and consulting firm. His award-winning blog, HealthBlawg, is highly regarded in both the legal and health policy blogging worlds. David is a charter member of the external Advisory Board of the Mayo Clinic Center for Social Media, and is a member of the advisory boards of FierceHealthIT and HealthWorks Collective. He serves as Public Policy Chair of the Society for Participatory Medicine. He is currently on the Health IT Standards Committee, Consumer Technology Workgroup (Office of the National Coordinator for Health IT, US Department of Health & Human Services). He speaks regularly before healthcare and legal industry groups on business, policy and legal matters.

Kamal Jethwani, MD, MPH leads the research and program evaluation initiatives at the Center for Connected Health as the corporate manager for research and innovation. He is an Assistant in Dermatology at Massachusetts General Hospital and Instructor at Harvard Medical School. His research is focused on technology-based models of health delivery and using behavior change as a tool for preventive and supportive care. His work at the Center has spanned designing and implementing clinical trials to leading efforts in predictive modeling using behavioral parameters. Dr. Jethwani is also responsible for shaping the research roadmap for the Center, leading the evaluation of all on-going programs, and contributing to efforts in the development and scaling of connected health programs.

Craig Kartchner, MBA is a marketing director for Intermountain Healthcare, an integrated hospital system based in Salt Lake City, Utah. Among his areas of focus are patient engagement, social media, mobile strategies, big data, and digital communications. Craig is an expert in healthcare social media, having led strategies that emphasize credible health content as the foundation for interacting with patients and helping them become engaged in their own care. Craig has an MBA from the University of Utah and has been with Intermountain for 12 years. He is actively involved in community volunteerism and leadership.

A. Jay Khanna, MD, MBA is a spine surgeon and Associate Professor in the Departments of Orthopedic Surgery and Biomedical Engineering at Johns Hopkins University. He is also the Director of the Johns Hopkins Orthopaedic and Spine Surgery practice in the Greater Washington region and sees patients in Bethesda, Maryland. He is actively involved in research and has written numerous peer-reviewed publications and book chapters on topics relating to spine surgery and has edited a popular textbook entitled *MRI for Orthopaedic Surgeons*. One of his greatest interests is education and he is the director of the annual American Academy of Orthopedic Surgeons Board Review Course and also directs several courses for the North American Spine Society and other organizations.

Andrew D. Rainey is the VP of Sales and Business Development at Binary Fountain. In this capacity, he is responsible for developing and executing business strategies for identifying, qualifying, and winning new business and building strategic partnerships. Mr. Rainey has helped leading organizations develop effective social media marketing strategies utilizing innovative tools and technologies, including Binary Fountain's PatientSI. Prior to joining Binary Fountain, Mr. Rainey provided global trade compliance consulting services and IT solutions to the aerospace and defense industry. He earned a BS in consumer economics and leadership from the University of Delaware. He and his wife reside in Fairfax, Virginia.

Rajesh K. Rajpal, MD is the founder of See Clearly Vision Group. Dr. Rajpal has served as Director of the Cornea and External Disease Service in the Department of Ophthalmology at Georgetown University as well as Director of the

Refractive Laser Eye Center at George Washington University Medical Center in Washington, D.C. He holds appointments on the clinical faculties of Georgetown University Medical Center and George Washington University Medical Center. His contributions in the field of ophthalmology span not only clinical care but also teaching, publishing, and clinical research. Dr. Rajpal is the author of numerous publications and abstracts as well as a frequently invited lecturer. He is a member of many ophthalmological societies, and served as President and on the Board of Directors of the Washington D.C. Ophthalmology Society and on the Board of Directors for Old Dominion Eye Bank.

Bryan Ross serves as the administrator of See Clearly Vision Group, a multi-location, multi-specialty eye care practice and management company in the Washington, DC metropolitan area. His 16-year eye care experience includes all aspects of practice management including billing and coding, reimbursement, government contracting, human resources, and regulatory/compliance issues. He has been with See Clearly Vision Group for more than 14 years. In his role as administrator he oversees the government contracting aspects of the military portion of the business as well as staff management care of the patients in multiple offices amd laser refractive surgery centers.

Stephen C Schimpff, MD, FACP is a quasi-retired internist and professor of medicine and public policy. He is a graduate of Rutgers University and Yale School of Medicine and is board certified in internal medicine, medical oncology and infectious disease. He previously served as COO of the University of Maryland Medical System and CEO of the University of Maryland Medical Center and is currently the chair of the advisory committee for Sanovas, Inc. and senior advisor to Sage Growth Partners. He is the author of *The Future of Medicine – Megatrends in Healthcare* and *The Future of Health Care Delivery – Why It Must Change and How It Will Affect You.* He has a Facebook page for his books, a Twitter handle of @drschimpff, and occasionally posts on YouTube and blogs at http://medicalmegatrends.blogspot.com.

Clarissa Schilstra is a student at Duke University and a two-time survivor of leukemia. Since entering remission in 2009, Clarissa has worked to channel her experiences as a patient to help other young cancer patients. She has served as a Johns Hopkins Pediatric Oncology Patient Ambassador, co-founded a support group for teenage cancer patients, and started a blog www.teen-cancer.com. Clarissa is the Vice-President of Blue Devils vs. Cancer, a student organization dedicated to raising funds and awareness for cancer research and cancer patients. She is a psychology major and hopes to attend medical school.

Adam Shapourian is the Public Relations and Digital Strategy Coordinator for Suburban Hospital, a member of Johns Hopkins Medicine. A resident of Rockville, Maryland, Mr. Shapourian has been employed at Suburban Hospital for 12 years, serving in various administrative and professional roles. He joined the marketing and communications department in 2011 and is responsible for social media strategy, curating online content and development for the hospital's website, search engine marketing for online campaigns, web analytics, design and development of microsites and blogs, as well as programming digital communications and anything else that falls under his "digital umbrella." A graduate of Towson University in Maryland, Mr. Shapourian holds a bachelor's degree in electronic media and is currently pursuing his master's degree in PR/corporate communications from Georgetown University.

John Sharp, MSSA, PMP, FHIMSS is the Senior Manager for Consumer Health IT at HIMSS. Previously he was Manager, Clinical Research Informatics at the Cleveland Clinic. He is also adjunct faculty in the Health Informatics Master's program at Kent State University. He has blogged about health IT since 2006 at ehealth.johnwsharp.com as well as for HealthWorksCollective.com where he is on the advisory board. He speaks nationally and internationally on social media in healthcare. He is a project management professional and a Fellow of HIMSS. John has chaired the eHealth SIG and participated in several committees and task forces including the local Northern Ohio chapter and the Clinical and Business Intelligence Working Group. He has also presented at HIMSS several times including panels on social media.

Susan Solomon, MA, MBA is vice president of marketing and communications for St. Joseph Health, a 16-hospital health system serving California, Texas, and New Mexico. In this role, she oversees branding, product line promotion, public relations, media relations, physician marketing, and all aspects of digital marketing. She is also a faculty member at four Southern California universities. Before joining St. Joseph Health, she was vice president of marketing and communications for Memorial Care in Southern California. She has addressed national and international audiences on new media and innovative marketing and public relations techniques. She is the author of the book *Building Powerful Health Care Brands* and has written more than 100 articles on new media for clickz.com and marketingprofs.com.

Brad Tritle, CIPP serves as Director of Business Development for Vitaphone health solutions, a patient monitoring and digital patient engagement firm focused on achieving improved outcomes, decreased costs, and an enhanced patient experience. He is a co-founder and advisor to eHealth Nexus, a company that enhances the value of Personal Health Record systems. Additionally, he serves on the advisory boards of the Health Record Banking Alliance, Ubora and Tiatros. Mr. Tritle is chair of the HIMSS Social Media Task Force, chair of the Health Record Banking Alliance Business Model and Promotional Committees, and is a co-author of the HIMSS book *Engage! Transforming Healthcare through Digital Patient Engagement*. He has served as a consultant to the Office of the

National Coordinator for Health IT, as well as to for-profit companies and non-profit organizations. Past positions include serving as CEO of eHealthTrust, Executive Director of Arizona Health-e Connection, and in multiple leadership positions for the State of Arizona government.

Jennifer K. Tweedy is a web and new media professional with 14 years of experience in the online space. She completed her undergraduate studies at the University of Illinois at Urbana-Champaign and holds a Master of Science in Technology from Arizona State University. Jennifer began her work in online media as a web designer in the private sector and over the course of her career has led teams of designers, developers, writers, and new media professionals. Jennifer is the Web & New Media Manager for the Arizona Department of Health Services (ADHS), where she launched the agency's social media efforts, is responsible for online community building strategy, and speaks on the use of social media in the public sector. ADHS has been recognized as an early adopter of online social media in Arizona state government and was named by MPHProgramsList.com as the #1 Most Friendly Social Media State Health Department for 2013. Reach Jennifer via email at jennifertweedy@gmail.com and on Twitter via @jennifertweedy.

Amita N. Vyas, PhD, is an Assistant Professor and Director of the Maternal and Child Health Program in the Department of Prevention and Community Health at The George Washington University School of Public Health and Health Services. Her decision to pursue a career in public health was spurred by her time in Calcutta working alongside Mother Teresa in the Missionaries of Charity. Today her work focuses on reproductive health care, adolescent health, and the health and development of immigrant children and adolescents. She holds an adjunct position in the Department of Population and Family Health Sciences at Johns Hopkins University Bloomberg School of Public Health. Her commitment to teaching was recognized recently as she received the Morton A. Bender Teaching Award from the George Washington University.

Jitendra Vyas is a co-founder and solutions evangelist for Binary Fountain. Prior to Binary Fountain, Jitendra co-founded zGraffiti, Inc. and Technology Ventures, a technical and management consulting firm. Jitendra is one of the co-founders of Avatar Capital, a private equity investment group. In 1999, Jitendra was selected for the *Who's Who Directory of International Information Technology Professionals*. Jitendra has held leadership positions in national non-profit organizations, including the Network of South Asian Professionals (NetSAP), The Indus Entrepreneurs (TIE), and Association for Computing Machinery. Jitendra holds a BS in computer science and engineering from the University of Toledo and an MS in business technologies from George Washington University. He resides in Mclean, Virginia with his wife and three children.

Shiyi Zan is a research analyst and coordinator at the Center for Connected Health and an Associate in Dermatology at Harvard Medical School. She currently participates in the creation and rigorous evaluation of technology-based solutions to transform the delivery of healthcare. She holds a BS in kinesiology from the University of Massachusetts, Amherst. Her current research specialty is in the use of social media for healthcare delivery in the adolescent and young adult population. Her research interests lie in the intersection of health, medicine, psychology, culture, policy, technology, and human-centered design. Follow her on Twitter: @shiyizan.

ACKNOWLEDGMENTS

The National Stroke Association granted permission to reproduce Figure 1-1.

Intermountain Healthcare provided Figures 112 and all figures in Chapter 6. They are used with permission. Copyright 2014 by Intermountain Healthcare.

Binary Fountain, Inc. granted permission to use the photos and charts in Chapter 3.

Suburban Hospital, Bethesda, Maryland, granted permission to use the hospital's name and images from its website in Chapter 5.

Children's Medical Center, Dallas, Texas granted permission to use images from Children's Patient and Family Network in Chapter 7.

The Arizona Department of Health Services granted permission to use images from its social media in Chapter 8.

Cleveland Clinic granted permission to use Figure 10-1. Copyright by Cleveland Clinic.

Seattle Children's Hospital granted permission to use Figure 10-2.

Boston Children's Hospital granted permission to use Figure 10-3.

The authors of Chapter 11 acknowledge the work of Meghan Searl, PhD, who conducted the focus group with teens to gather data on their attitudes regarding using Facebook to find and share information about their health and asthma. We summarize some of the key findings from the focus group in this chapter. We also want to acknowledge the work of the staff at the Center for Connected Health who worked on this study and at the Partners Human Research Committee who assisted with the IRB review and approval process.

Contents

Foreword

The Future of Social Media in Healthcare

Stephen C. Schimpff, MD, FACP

Social media is all about sharing information. It involves networking and sharing with a group of like-minded individuals with similar interests. Increasingly, it is becoming the primary method by which people communicate and most likely will be the major media of tomorrow. We learn from each other and prefer to engage in two-way rather than one-way communication. Such interaction makes the communication social.

In less than a decade, the Yellow Pages have become almost obsolete, supplanted by internet searching and increasingly by social media. Not surprisingly, people who engage with social media via the telephone, texting, Facebook, Twitter®, LinkedIn®, YouTube, and blogs want to use social media in the healthcare arena as well.

Surveys now show that more than 40% of respondents indicate that social media information affects how they deal with their health. That already impressive number is likely to grow quickly. Younger adults use social media more than their older counterparts, and they have sufficiently tight social networks to believe they can trust the information obtained there. Many individuals now use social networks to garner information about the best doctor for a specific problem or the nearest hospital with a needed clinical program. Smart phone applications are proliferating rapidly, with more than 20% of users having at least one app. Among healthcare providers, social media has become a major method for professional networking, often using LinkedIn. Doctors are beginning to appreciate the value of social media to educate patients and families on upcoming surgery, procedure, and treatment plans. Hospitals use social media for marketing and to assess patient satisfaction.

This book contains the latest information and perspectives on social media in healthcare. The invited authors are from leading healthcare institutions and have demonstrated their expertise in the social media arena. The editor, Christina Thielst, FACHE, is highly regarded in the field and, hence, was asked by HIMMS to produce this volume. Among institutions represented are Dallas Children's Hospital, Surburban Hospital, St Joseph Health System, Intermountain Health System, Cleveland Clinic, and a team from the Center for Connected Health, Massachusetts General Hospital and Harvard Medical School. Others include healthcare lawyer and blogger David Harlow, Jennifer K. Tweedy of the Arizona Department of Health Services, general surgeon David Gleber, Brad Tritle, volunteer chairperson of the HIMSS Social Media Task Force, healthcare IT evangelist Brian Ahier and a collective sample of ambulatory care providers. Offering a patient perspective is Clarissa Schilstra, who has battled acute leukemia twice and made excellent use of social media to help herself and many others. If you are looking for the most up-to-date and complete compendium on social media in healthcare, you need look no further.

Humans depend on each other to learn. In early schooling, communication is largely unidirectional from teacher to student, but as we age, our learning becomes more interactive. Social media provides a great platform for faster, more in-depth interactions. Because such communication can occur in discontinuous time, participants need not be concurrently available and "on line," as with the telephone or face-to-face communication. Social media allows large numbers of people to interact, add to their knowledge, and ask questions.

Healthcare lags in the use of social media compared to other sectors, perhaps because it is a more conservative discipline and must respect important privacy issues. However, social media is not a passing fad; it is fast becoming the "norm" for communication. Accordingly, healthcare professionals should embrace it now, or they will definitely be behind the power curve.

Patients use the internet more than any other source for health information – for better or worse and evidence-based or not. They also use it to communicate with family and friends regarding health issues; to connect with groups (communities) of others who have the same illness; and, to a lesser degree to date, to interact with their healthcare providers.

Social media has been a boon to communication among patients. They join or create information exchanges about rare or terrifying diseases. They develop virtual support groups to learn how others handle, for example, the rigors of cancer chemotherapy, such as the loss of hair, the fatigue, and the isolation. Patients also rate their doctors and hospitals via social media. The old adage that "a happy customer will tell someone, but an unhappy one will tell ten others" is magnified logarithmically with social media. Increasingly, patients expect their physicians, nurse practitioners, and other providers to communicate digitally, definitely by email, increasingly by texting, and perhaps via Skype® or other tele-media techniques. Such communication can save a visit to the office or prevent a trip to the emergency department.

Every patient seeks information from his or her provider, who understandably has a higher level of knowledge about healthcare, but the patient needs and wants their provider to level the information playing field. Social media can both meet that need and save the physician time. For example, a blog post or video can help to prepare all patients scheduled for a knee replacement, augmented by direct communication for patient-specific details. Patients want communication quickly, competently, completely, and often confidentially. Most people want connections, and social media can establish them, reserving highly confidential information for direct interaction. Providers can save substantial time, patients can gain more knowledge than they might with more traditional forms of communication, and this direct conversation can be repeated as often as needed for the patient to understand the information fully. The end product is a more satisfied patient who, because he or she is more knowledgeable, should be a "better" patient, with greater understanding of the diagnosis and treatment plan and potentially greater compliance with recommendations.

Patients, especially elderly patients, should make an effort to connect online. That's where the information is, and people who don't take advantage of the technology could lose out. So, if you have elderly parents or grandparents, take the time to teach them about social media and how to find the information they need.

Social media users like the transparency of the process and the sharing effect, which can be disconcerting to providers when they discover negative comments or ratings. This underlines the importance of anticipating situations and handling any negativity immediately. Providers need to address all negative comments and resolve the issues quickly.

Although social media has become a rapidly growing tool for organizational providers (e.g., hospitals, pharmaceutical firms, physical therapy offices), providers have not yet maximized its full potential. In addition to their websites, hospitals now almost routinely have a Twitter handle and a Facebook page to communicate with their patients. For example, the Cleveland Clinic created its "Health Hub" as a one-stop portal that includes social media outlets. The result is many thousands of Twitter followers and even more Facebook fans. Physicians are slowly jumping on board.

Specialty centers can do the same, with messages going out to all patients or anyone who might be interested in their services. An integrative medicine center might, for example, include their own materials as well as messages from Dr. Andrew Weil, a classically trained physician who focuses on the use of complementary methods for addressing health while still committed to scientific principles, or Dr. Mark Hyman, another traditionally trained physician who has focused on the fundamental causes of chronic illnesses, most of which emanate from personal adverse behaviors related to eating, exercise, stress, and tobacco. In addition, the center may include information about healthy foods and the value of yoga or tai chi.

Social media can serve as a good medium to address the obesity epidemic in the United States. Research has shown that people are more likely to stay on a path of healthy diet and exercise when part of a group. Social media allow the group to interact at any time and any place without being dependent on a physical location and specific time.

Generally, physicians have been slow to adopt the use of social media in their professional lives. One exception is Howard Luks, MD, who has a blog that contains solid evidence-based information (http://www.howardluksmd.com/blog/). Dr. Luks notes that the blog makes his patients better informed when they arrive for a visit. Physicians can and a few do send general information via public social media, such as Facebook or YouTube, but not person-specific details.

My primary care physician has a Facebook page, mostly containing general information, such as "it's time to get your flu shot" or a reminder of the benefits of exercise, but it is not very specific. Some physicians use Facebook to send general thoughts to their patients. A primary care physician might post regularly about diet or exercise, why vitamin D is important in northern latitudes, or how to slow the process of aging. Specialists might direct their posts to items specific to their specialty. Few physicians use Twitter to communicate with patients, and few have even considered producing videos for YouTube. This landscape is changing. Newly graduated doctors, pharmacists, nurses, physical therapists, dentists, and others are long accustomed to social media and not daunted by using it to communicate with patients. Kevin Pho, MD, a primary care physician, has a blog (http://www.kevinmd.com/blog/) that has become the most viewed medical blog, filled with not only his posts but guest posts as well. He suggests that physicians overcome their reluctance to using this form of communication. More specifically, he suggests that physicians embrace social media because that is where patients get information. It is incumbent upon physicians to be sure the information available through social media is accurate, such as the efficacy and safety of vaccines.

Social media can be used for improving patient satisfaction. For example, if the doctor is running late, a text message can advise patients to come to the office later than scheduled. This obviously avoids a waiting room full of cranky patients and shows patients that they are considered "valued customers."

Medical students, more attuned to social media than older physicians, have used Facebook, Twitter, or texting for instant celebrations on senior "Match Day." Such announcements create excitement and spread the emotion of the moment to friends and families, who can then respond immediately and be part of the excitement. Some deans have begun to use Facebook, Twitter, or blogs to communicate with students as never before. Such communication makes the dean much more approachable and has given students a sense of connection that simply could not exist in the past. Further, because students can respond, the dean receives instant feedback on thoughts, ideas, and plans.

In recent in-depth interviews with many primary care physicians, I found that only a few use email to communicate with patients because there is no reimbursement for such time. Others are comfortable with email requests for prescription refills or simple questions that do not require urgent responses. However, they do not want patients using email as a primary means of communicating because it loses the nuances of a face-to-face or even a telephone conversation. A few have Facebook pages that contain general information, but none invite their patients to be their friends on their personal Facebook page. None that I interviewed are now using Twitter or YouTube. However, as Dr. Pho points out, social media is where the patients are, so physicians also need to be there or lose their influence.

A big question in the arena of social media is whether it can be used to help redesign the currently dysfunctional healthcare delivery system. Critical to this endeavor is whether knowledgeable individuals, including physicians, nurses, and other providers, become engaged. If they do not, the field will be left to well-meaning but uninformed individuals who may not appreciate how to provide appropriate medical care for best outcomes.

Where is social media going in healthcare? Far be it for me to venture an answer other than to observe that social media has grown by leaps and bounds and will certainly continue to do so. No doubt there will be new platforms, not yet dreamed of, to challenge the current platforms. More providers and patients will interact with each other via social media. That much of the future can be predicted, but much else is speculation.

Preface

Christina Beach Thielst, FACHE

My blogging journey began in 2005 after attending a presentation by one of the world's top bloggers, Doc Searls, on blogs, wiki, and pings at our local city college. The presentation instantly solved my dilemma about whether I, a hospital administrator turned consultant, should create a website. For a few years I had considered and even started to work on a website, but the static nature just didn't feel right. In contrast, a blog allowed me to share information and knowledge and interact with others, which was a much better fit with my character and professional branding.

As I continued to learn about the technologies and watched social media unfold, I couldn't help but envision how these tools could be applied in healthcare environments, especially after I returned to a hospital Chief Operating Officer role. Having twice been a risk manager and charged with ensuring compliance, I also began identifying and considering the risks and evaluating the safeguards for social media to minimize damage and losses.

A couple of health information exchange/regional health information organization friends were blogging, and soon my blogroll included The Healthcare IT Guy, eHealth, Candid CIO, HIStalk, Healthcare IT Blog, Clinicore, Family Medicine Notes, The Health Care Blog, Health Is Social, and EMR & HIPAA. A few of us even planned the first blogger meet-ups at the Health Information and Management Systems Society Annual Conference, which have now evolved into an elaborate Social Media Center.

Nearly 10 years later, look how far we have come. Healthcare social media isn't just a few information technology guys, a couple of clinicians, and an administrator or two who use their voices, connect, and collaborate virtually. Today, social media is part of the business of healthcare and most importantly has transformed into important patient and family caregiver tools.

Brad Tritle ends his chapter in *Engage, Transforming Healthcare Through Digital Patient Engagement* with a review of why social media matters. For patients, he points to the importance of meeting them "where they are." For the healthcare system, he states "Social media brings highly effective communication channels and functionality into an industry, healthcare, that requires more effective ways for participants to engage with each other with great potential to enhance the provider-patient relationship."

To attain the vision of a new healthcare delivery system and the goals that have been set in place for a new approach to medicine, we must adopt the right tools, for the right purpose, and the right audience. Only when we are both effective and efficient in our communications and engagement of consumers will we truly have an impact on the health of populations at a cost we can afford.

I encourage you to look around your profession and organization with open eyes and consider the opportunities of social technologies for connecting, communicating, collaborating … and engaging!

Chapter 1:

Introduction

Christina Beach Thielst, FACHE

#SOCIALBIZ

The business of healthcare is a conservative one and rightly so. There is great risk associated with avenues of communications and care is taken to ensure appropriate safeguards and privacy. As in other industries, healthcare social media really began with basic marketing and public relations. The growing use of social channels like Facebook and Twitter® offered healthcare marketers new avenues of access to audiences for their marketing materials and public communications. They soon partnered with their organizations' web teams to integrate social media with their public websites and cross-promote content and connections. As traditional media outlets continued to struggle to maintain their audiences, healthcare marketing and communications professionals found that new social channels, such as Google+, Foursquare, Twitter, Instagram®, and Pinterest, could provide more targeted outreach.

Social networks and technologies could not be held captive by the marketing and communications staff or the web team. Physicians, nurses, technicians, and even a few administrators began to envision how these tools could improve care processes and the patient's experience. They soon began adopting social media and technologies to address patient care and safety challenges in both healthcare settings and patient homes. The drive to transform the healthcare delivery system to accommodate changes introduced by the Patient Protection and Affordable Care Act and demanded by aging Baby Boomers is about to push social technologies to the forefront of conversations on increasing efficiency and self-management tools.

Social channels are becoming ever more integrated into our lives, and today's empowered consumers increasingly expect healthcare service providers and insurers to maintain a social presence and meet them on their preferred channels. Social platforms are now common in many workplaces in an effort to improve communications and support virtual collaboration among individuals, teams, and committees. Recruiters increasingly reach out to healthcare professionals on social networks to identify candidates for open positions and to promote the work environment and culture.

Professionals now realize that success in the business of healthcare requires incorporation of these tools and recognition of the value propositions offered by the numerous media channels. Hospitals, clinics, and individual professionals have correctly saved the best for last and are increasingly finding innovative applications for these technologies to better engage consumers, patients, and their family caregivers in care processes.

Healthcare professionals have also realized that shutting down social media does not manage the risks; it only pushes them out of sight, where they can fester until harm is done. Managing the risks inherent with any mode of communication requires leadership and starts with building knowledge, engaging, and adjusting based upon feedback. The need is to meet customers where they are and give them the tools they need for better management of their own care and the care of others in their family.

Social media technologies and branded media are maturing and becoming acceptable tools and are going beyond educational awareness in the business of healthcare. These include:

Social Intelligence: Collecting and analyzing posts, images shared, status updates, comments, conversations, "likes," "tips," and more from social channels about attitudes, perceptions, and behaviors as they relate to the organization's brand and trends.

Social Customer Relationship Management: Leveraging intelligence gathered to create digital profiles of individuals for more personalized information and interactions with consumers, patients, donors, and other stakeholder groups.

Clinical Trials and Research: Promotion of clinical trials and targeted recruitment of candidates on social media and within key networks as well as serving as a platform for research activities.

Social Surveillance: Analyzing posts to identify food-borne illness and disease outbreaks, natural disasters, man-made emergencies, and other public health concerns.

Social Advertising and Fundraising: Optimizing the social connections that have been built over time and targeting advertising or donor outreach with engaging content.

Social Gaming: Entertaining games that include social networking components to help consumers change behaviors and achieve targeted health benefits.

Care Coordination and Facilitation of Patient Transitions: Platforms for communications between service provider and patient, exchange of information, accessing peer support, and monitoring health status across the entire care continuum.

The blending of social tools with each of the previously described business functions brings everyone closer to the ultimate goal of *improving a population's health* and shifts the paradigm away from a focus on treating individual episodes of illness to improving the overall health of populations.[1] Social technologies are a complement to existing health information technology systems and help providers maintain contact with patients, especially those who have complex care needs or multiple chronic conditions, before, during, and after their treatment encounters. Such contact can be used to:

- Assess risks
- Track patients by population
- Update patient status
- Monitor adherence to treatment plans and care guidelines
- Coordinate care across multiple settings
- Intervene when necessary

Consider the following examples of healthcare organizations using social technologies to improve the health of targeted populations[2] and the potential impact on access, quality and cost.

- Boston Medical Center's use of an avatar to conduct a pre-conception assessment of teens at risk for poor reproductive health and family planning outcomes
- United Health Centers of San Joaquin's use of a social networking platform to help safety-net providers and patients manage chronic disease
- Partners HealthCare's use of texting for reminders and prevention messaging with multiple populations to realize improvements in adherence to care plans, decreases in "no show" rates and sustained behavior change
- Boston Children's use of social media to augment traditional surveillance methods of hypoglycemia in diabetes to expand knowledge of complications and impact behaviors
- Children's Hospital Dallas's secure online social networking community for patient and family peer support
- Nemours/Alfred I DuPont Hospital for Children's using a secure social enterprise network to collect real-time feedback from family advisors
- Aetna's use of a social networking platform to support beneficiaries recovering from addiction and to help prioritize case manager outreach activities

HEALTH LITERACY AND SAFETY

Social technologies can also facilitate evidence-based strategies, such as closed-loop communications, and create trails of documentation for monitoring and analysis. They can complement the information available to patients from their electronic health records (EHRs) with more patient-centric content that is understandable and actionable, even for those with low health literacy. An estimated 77 million people in the United States have a poor understanding of basic medical vocabulary and are often the people at greatest risk of medical complications and hospital readmission.[3]

Social technologies easily accommodate audio, video, simulated environments, and graphics that can engage consumers and patients by minimizing the need for long text full of medical vocabulary that is often written at too high a reading level. Infographics can convey information clearly and concisely (Figs 1-1 and 1-2), and they are easily accommodated by social media, thus supporting health literacy.

A recent personal experience highlights the role of social media in increasing the health literacy for everyone, even health professionals. After suffering from knee pain and not benefiting from attempts to resolve it, I had an MRI that indicated a medial meniscus tear. While I nervously waited the few days before my appointment with an orthopedist, I did what any other baby boomer would do and

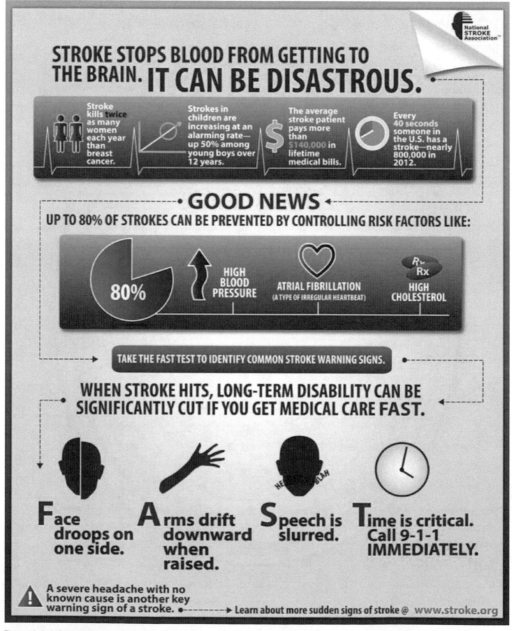

Figure 1-1. Infographic on stroke prevention and recognition. © 2013 National Stroke Association. Content provided by permission of National Stroke Association. Please visit www.stroke.org for stroke education resources.

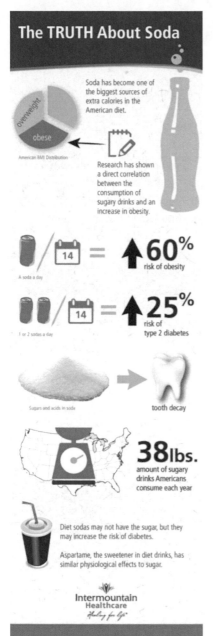

Figure 1-2. Infographic on links between soda and medical conditions. From Intermountain Healthcare.

used Google to search on my diagnosis to see what I could find. The top result of my search was a blog post by a physician I had spoken with while preparing to write this book. Dr. Luks believes videos, and social media in general, humanize his practice and communicate information that might otherwise consume valuable time during appointments.[4]

Dr. Luks is a Chief of Sports Medicine and Arthroscopy on the East Coast and his post was titled "Meniscus Tears... Why surgery isn't always necessary." I found the information, pictures and video contained in the post to be extremely helpful in providing me with some baseline information on my diagnosis and options. During the appointment, here on the West Coast, I was comforted to hear from my surgeon a suggested plan that aligned with what I had learned from Dr. Luks' blog post. The insight and improvement in my own health literacy helped me ask more productive questions and very quickly make the decision for treatment that was needed.

OPPORTUNITIES FOR INNOVATION

Social technologies offer tremendous opportunities for innovation and new approaches to the way care is experienced. The best positioned healthcare organizations recognize this and will:

- Use social tools to advance their goals and mission
- Harness the collective wisdom of staff and broaden collaboration
- Recognize needs of patients and their family caregivers
- Change how care is provided and offer online engagement opportunities that are designed with the user in mind
- Use enterprise-wide portals to integrate social tools with other patient-facing systems, such as the EHR and patient education
- Manage their online reputations

The case studies contained in this book reflect innovative thinking and examples from healthcare organizations that have chosen to position themselves to meet the challenges of new healthcare demands. As you read through the case studies and chapters, think about the triple aims of the Centers for Medicare & Medicaid Services and how social tools can help to:

- Improve the health of the populations
- Improve the care delivery experience
- Keep healthcare affordable

REFERENCES

1. Thielst C. Social technologies: meeting the challenges of population health. *Patient Safety & Quality Healthcare*. Online First. 2013. http://www.psqh.com/online-first/1752-social-technologies-meeting-the-challenges-of-population-health.html. Accessed November 18, 2013.

2. http://www.psqh.com/online-first/1752-social-technologies-meeting-the-challenges-of-population-health.html.

3. http://www.ihealthbeat.org/perspectives/leveraging emerging technologies for improved patient engagement and safety.

4. Oldenburg J, Chase D, Christensen K, Tritle B. *Engage! Transforming Healthcare through Digital Patient Engagement*. Chicago, IL: HIMSS; 2013.

Chapter 2:

The Value of Social Media: A Patient's Perspective

Clarissa Schilstra

Editor's note: *Social media can have a major impact on patients, their families, and their friends. In sharing her story, Clarissa Schilstra, a 19-year-old cancer survivor, describes how social media can be one of the most beneficial resources available for a person going through a severe illness, such as cancer. Social media and internet tools can link patients and survivors, providing much-needed personal support online. The technologies facilitate support groups, information sharing and other online resources that provide patients with the tools to overcome isolation. They can also serve as a jumping-off point for patients to take action to solve the problems they are facing and help others facing those same challenges.*

FACING A DIFFICULT DIAGNOSIS

I am a 19-year-old cancer survivor. I was initially diagnosed with acute lymphoblastic leukemia (ALL) at 2½ years old. Although I successfully completed treatment and went into remission, I faced a relapse 10 years later, when I was 13 years old. Overnight, I went from being a childhood cancer survivor with a bright future to a teenage cancer patient facing a less than 40% chance of survival.

Overcoming Isolation

After my relapse diagnosis, I experienced many emotions and challenges, but the feeling of isolation was unquestionably the most powerful and had the greatest impact on my life. I felt like I was in a little boat all by myself in the middle of a vast ocean. In that little boat, I was doing everything I could to survive, while everyone else my age was on a giant cruise ship right next to me, having fun and enjoying life. It was all right there around me, where I could see it and hear about it, but I could never reach it. My treatment prevented me from being part of it. The worst part of the whole situation was that almost no resources were available to help teens with cancer, like myself, through the social and emotional struggles of the isolated life of a cancer patient with no energy or immune system.

Fortunately, at least a few online resources and social media outlets provided me with a way to combat my isolation. My biggest helper during treatment was the website CarePages (www.carepages.com). My mom set up a personal blog for me on CarePages and kept our family and friends updated with regular postings. My father's family is from the Netherlands, and they were able to access CarePages to follow my progress from far away. We could keep the posts private through the settings that CarePages offered, enabling access only to those whom we allowed through the CarePages member request system. However, we had the opportunity to make the page open to other CarePages members so that others going through a similar illness could contact us.

Writing the blog proved a crucial outlet for my mom, giving her a place to process everything that I went through and to share her own thoughts and feelings. More importantly, it saved us all an enormous amount of time and energy by automatically sending out updates to everyone following our page, so that we did not have to make the repeated phone calls or emails that would have otherwise been necessary. She often posted daily updates, especially during the most difficult times of my treatment. I would like to share a segment from one of her blog posts to illustrate how the blog offered outsiders a window into the difficult world of a cancer patient.

> "The drip begins so innocently. A clear fluid that looks like water in a glass bottle. The nurse attaches it to the port line that runs right into Clarissa's heart vein. The drip begins. I watch as my smiling daughter becomes paler and paler. Her smile begins to get smaller. Eventually, it is replaced by a look of hollowness, a look of discomfort, bordering on pain. There is a pallor that comes over her face as her body accepts the toxic medicine and the chemo kills the good as well as the bad cells. Why can't there be a cure that allows just the bad cells to be attacked? She begins to curl up, almost in the fetal position. There is no way to ease the nausea in her stomach. Clarissa dozes off into a light sleep. Escaping from the misery of the chemo through sleep is brought abruptly to an end by the relentless beep, beep, beep of the machine holding the bags of hydration fluid hanging on the IV pole. Her eyes open and the pain is evident across her pale and strained face. Where does this child get her courage, as we begin a new day and start this routine all over again? I keep telling Clarissa, only four more days, only three more days, only two more days, and then finally, only one more day."

CarePages also helped to raise my family's spirits by providing a message board on which friends and family posted messages of encouragement, giving us that little extra push to fight on. In the first year of my relapse treatment, more than 50 people posted a total of 350 messages in response to my parents' Carepages posts. My mother and I looked forward to reading each one after it was posted. For us, it felt like a lifeline to the outside world. It is easy to become despondent when isolated in a hospital room for days and weeks at a time. The words of encouragement and support that we received on CarePages gave us the strength and hope to stay positive. My mother always said that the single biggest weapon of a cancer patient is a positive attitude. The following are examples of some of the responses we received:

> 7/30/2007
>
> Hi Clarissa. You are doing such a great job fighting the bad guys. Thanks for posting, Chris, it really helps us understand - we think about you often and admire all of your strength, courage, and faith. Love, xxxx

> 12/18/2007
>
> You've been an inspiration to all of us that have been following your ordeal these past months. I'm continually amazed by your immediate and community family's love and support. Your story is another bright star in this Christmas sky. Merry Christmas and a happy and healthy New Year!

My mother and I also posted pictures on my CarePages that showed people how I looked along my journey through the cancer treatment. At the end of my treatment, my parents chose the CarePages option to print a hardcover book of all the blog posts, messages, and pictures throughout my treatment. My mother still looks at my CarePages Keepsake book to remind herself of the adversity we have overcome as a family.

While my family used CarePages to update our extended family and friends on my progress, I know of other families who used Facebook to keep loved ones updated. One family made a Facebook page for their daughter and posted on it weekly. Along with the updates, they created events linked to her page, which they used for the fundraisers they held to help with the cost of her treatment.

Whether patients choose CarePages or similar sites like CaringBridge (www. caringbridge.org/), these resources are key in helping patients find others going through similar experiences. In my case, CarePages helped me to find survivors of a leukemia relapse to whom I could reach out. The site offered a search tool I could use to search for "leukemia" and "relapse" to find other patients' pages. I found two girls my age who had also gone through an ALL relapse. I contacted them through email and they responded. I became pen pal friends with both of them as I went through the last year of my treatment. They both helped me immensely, providing me with advice and simply commiserating with me at particularly difficult times. Sharing my experiences, however bad they may have been, with someone who had been through similar challenges made me feel significantly less isolated. Their support continues to help me now that I am done with my treatment. Because they warned me about the late effects they experienced, I am aware of symptoms and problems I may face post-treatment.

Facebook, email, texts, phone calls, or video chats were also great ways for me to keep in touch with my friends from school. Those tools for staying connected were especially useful during the long weeks I was trapped in the hospital or in my bed at home.

Although contact relieved my feeling of isolation, it also gnawed at me with the details of all I was missing. The best example of this occurred the weekend of homecoming during my sophomore year, when I was nearing the end of my treatment. The swine flu hit my school. So close to successfully completing my chemotherapy, my parents and I decided it would not be smart to risk my catching the flu and that it would be best for me not to attend homecoming. While it was wonderful that my friends shared all their photos with me on Facebook and let me know how much they wished I could have been there, it also made me sad to think about all of the fun I missed.

The connections I maintained with my friends meant the most to me when I prepared to go back to high school, a little more than halfway through tenth grade, after 2 years of home schooling. Those friends with whom I had remained connected were the ones who helped me to get used to being in school again and to get from class to class. In the grand scheme of things, social media and other forms of online communication were, undoubtedly, more often a blessing than a curse.

Surviving Cancer

Facebook and email have enabled me to stay in touch with the amazing doctors and nurses who saved my life. As a survivor, there is nothing I love more than finding a "Happy Birthday" message in my Facebook inbox from the oncologist who held my hand to comfort me as he told me of my relapse. I also use Facebook to celebrate each year I am cancer-free, posting a baldheaded photo of myself during treatment to commemorate my end of chemo and a message of thanks for the support that has led to my continued survival. Taking that time to remember what I went through and sharing my gratitude for all those who supported me keeps me focused on doing as much good with my life as possible.

Feeling so grateful to be alive and healthy, I became incredibly determined to do something to make sure that other teens with cancer would not have to feel as alone and different as I did while fighting for their lives. In a discussion with my parents and a teacher at my school, I decided to embark on a research project to develop an outline for a book to help teens with cancer through the social and emotional challenges of treatment. I wanted to focus on the issues that had given me such a hard time. Because I had been so dissatisfied with the few resources I had found, I thought this would be a great way to create an easily accessible resource for others going through all that I had experienced. However, by the time I had finished all of the necessary research, put together an outline, and got everything in order to write a book, I was feeling completely better and wanted to get back to my "normal" life again.

Luckily, before abandoning my book plan, I had the opportunity to meet with Dr. Stephen C. Schimpff, the author of the Foreword to this book and the author of several other books on healthcare. With his help, I came up with the idea to write a blog to organize all of my thoughts for the book while gaining readership.

By doing a little research, I found a software and a hosting system with which I could develop my website. After building it entirely on my own and writing up my first post, I launched www.teen-cancer.com. My blog began as a simple way to share my coping strategies with other teen patients and survivors, but it grew to become an amazing healing mechanism for me and a tool to connect with other young people going through cancer treatment.

Shortly after beginning my blog, I had the opportunity to become a Patient Ambassador for Johns Hopkins Pediatric Oncology, which gave me many opportunities to share my story and my blog. The best part was that as a Patient Ambassador, I have a "Meet Clarissa" page on the Johns Hopkins website, which shares my story and includes the link to my blog at http://www.hopkinsmedicine.org/ kimmel_cancer_center/centers/pediatric_oncology/patient_stories/clarissa.html.

To track my readership after these first publicity opportunities, I researched website trackers and found that Google Analytics was a simple and easily installed tool to help me track my website traffic. After installing it, I was so gratified to see the jumps in traffic to my site from all around the world. I was even contacted by a librarian in England, who was compiling an online medical resource library for cancer patients and requested permission to include my blog in her site.

The longer I kept up my posts, the more I wanted to enhance my site with multimedia. I added a photos page to share all of the pictures from my treatment with readers, so they could see what happened to me throughout that difficult time and know that they were not the only ones losing their hair or dealing with their scars. Along with the pictures, I incorporated a resources page to share helpful videos and links to information. I included links to websites like Teens Living With Cancer, which I had found particularly useful as a place to read about the challenges other patients and survivors faced. I also shared two of my posts on the website www.kevinmd.com, a popular blog maintained by a doctor and displaying the writing of both patients and healthcare providers.

Going into my fourth year of writing my blog and having my website, I can say that the most rewarding aspect has been the emails from the readers who were patients like me. I have received so many emails from parents and teens, filled with questions, requests for additional information, or words of thanks. It is these responses that motivate me to continue to do what I can to provide resources to young people facing cancer. Furthermore, I attribute my acceptance to Duke University, in great part, to what I have achieved with internet tools and social media avenues.

All of this involvement with online resources spurred me on to develop a support group for teen cancer patients and survivors with the help of one of my friends, also a cancer survivor, who I had met in the hospital. Not entirely sure where to begin in our quest to develop such a group, my friend and I got in touch with a local organization called Cool Kids Campaign, which supports children with cancer and their families. Cool Kids provided us with a space, activities, and food with which we could host an event. We created a name and logo to grow our group. As teenagers, we knew that Facebook would be the best place for us to start. We built our group a Facebook page and created a Facebook event to invite other patients and survivors, specifically those we had met through our treatments at Johns Hopkins, to our first teens.CanSur.vive (https://www.facebook.com/groups/teens.CanSur.vive/) meeting.

Our first support group meeting was a great success and we have had many others since then. Although our support group is not necessarily group therapy, it is a place where teens can get together and talk about anything from hospital food to long-term treatment effects to school. Our goal with teens.CanSur.vive is to give all teens with cancer a place to share their stories. There is something incredibly therapeutic about spending time complaining, laughing, joking, and crying about stories of chemo, ports, spinal taps, radiation, doctors, allergic reactions, nurses, operations, challenges, school, friends, and the crazy life of a teen with cancer!

Each time we want to host a teens.CanSur.vive meeting, we use Facebook to create an event and spread the word. More importantly, Facebook has allowed our group members to stay connected throughout the year regardless of where they go to school. When one of our friends lost her fight or when another relapsed, we were able to pull together and support each other, whether we did so virtually or in person.

Social Media Accessibility

As a young adult who has had more than her fair share of experiences in the world of healthcare, I am grateful that I had access to social media resources during my treatment. Had I not had my own laptop or access to the internet during my many weeks in the hospital, I would never have been able to keep in touch with my friends at home or find the few support resources available for teenagers going through cancer treatment. I believe it is imperative for all hospitals and clinics to provide patients with access to such online resources, whether through a simple internet connection for those who have their own devices or by providing patients with electronic devices, such as tablets, to gain access to online resources.

Healthcare providers can do much more to teach patients about the online resources available to them and, in some cases, how to use them. For example, the social worker assigned to my case at Johns Hopkins Hospital told me and my family about CarePages shortly after I was diagnosed, citing it as a great tool to keep family and friends updated on my progress. We would never have known about this valuable resource had she not taken the time to explain it to us.

I am a huge proponent of psychological support for patients battling severe illness, and I think social media sites such as CarePages and online group support forums, as well as tools such as blogs, offer patients immediate access to emotional and social support. There is no better therapy than hearing words of encouragement from loved ones or taking time to commiserate with someone going through a similar hardship. Such access is mutually beneficial to patients and providers because it results in more satisfied, supported patients as well as the opportunity for patients to foster long-term friendships with the providers who play an integral role in saving their lives.

Knowing that patients have such tools to overcome their challenges is unbelievably encouraging. I very much look forward to seeing more young adults who are facing significant health-related obstacles participate in developing more patient-centered and patient-founded resources, both in print and electronically, in the coming years.

Chapter 3:

Social Intelligence About The Patient Experience

Andrew Rainey; Jitendra Vyas; A. Jay Khanna, MD, MBA; Kashif Firozvi, MD; Rajesh Rajpal, MD; Amita Vyas, PhD; Bryan Ross

Social media has created an incredible venue for consumers and patients to share experiences and perceptions related to health services. Although most healthcare organizations and practices know the importance of understanding patient satisfaction, they require new approaches to quantify, analyze, and interpret the sea of patient feedback they are obtaining from social media. Distilling these patient insights represents the first step in better management and delivery of services.

The use of social media has grown to 62% worldwide and 75% in the United States, fundamentally transforming how we learn, act, and collaborate. In 2012, there were 1.5 billion combined users of online social media sites such as Facebook and Twitter®. These users contributed to more than 500 million Facebook likes and 340 million tweets per day.[1] Social media has become embedded in the operations of organizations in nearly every market, including healthcare. The healthcare industry is currently experiencing a massive transformation; the traditional referral-based approaches to attract and retain patients are being challenged by social media and healthcare review sites. Patients are increasingly turning to social media review sites to learn about providers and healthcare facilities. A HRI survey found that 42% of consumers are using social media to access health-related consumer reviews. Further, social media has now opened the door for two-way online communication between providers and patients, which will have a profound effect on patient experiences and ultimately on both health outcomes and organizational revenues.

FEEDBACK TRANSFORMED (OR 2.0)

Social media has empowered patients as never before. Previously, if patients were dissatisfied with their providers, they may have indicated their disappointment on a feedback card and possibly shared their experiences with a few friends, suggesting that they not use services at that facility. These same dissatisfied patients now use diverse online communication platforms, mobile technologies, and social media. Patients not only can share their opinions and experiences *immediately* using these platforms, but their voices have an enormous reach. Each channel and medium has lowered the "hurdle" to providing feedback. Instead of finding a feedback card or caring enough to fill out a survey, patients can quickly and easily share their experiences with the world.

With today's universal availability of a blog or a tweet, a disgruntled patient can negatively taint the reputation of a top-tier physician, well-known hospital,

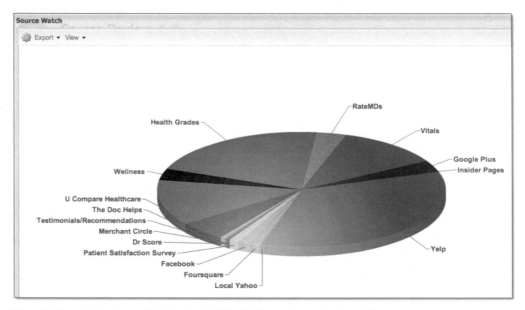

Figure 3-1: Sample Distribution of Insights by Social Media/Review Source for a Hospital

or practice. This is a time of disproportionate reward and retribution. Hospitals, practices, and physicians who are not aware of their online reputations or the influence of social media are vulnerable and at a distinct disadvantage. Rather than simply being aware of their online presence, healthcare organizations must have a well-defined plan and process to harvest, analyze, and interpret these new data sources.

At present, customer satisfaction-focused organizations are struggling to harvest and understand the thousands of social media sources and millions of unstructured social feedback conversations. Most organizations do not have the capacity to analyze/distill/understand social feedback for its implications on their business operations.

Adding to the mix is the mandate from the Centers for Medicare & Medicaid Services (CMS) for regulatory compliance by hospitals for variable payments based on quality of service and the patient experience. This trend is likely to continue as the Patient Protection and Affordable Care Act includes language requiring CMS to create a web portal featuring data on the comparative performances of physicians as well as patient ratings for physicians and providers. Patient experience could now drive reimbursement at the level of the payer. The Hospital Consumer Assessment of Healthcare Providers and Systems (HCAHPS) survey is the first national publicly reported, standardized survey of patient impressions of hospital care. Providers and hospitals must be aligned to ensure that their patients not only receive excellent care but that their perceptions of that care upon discharge are superior to that of their respective peers. The regulated oversight of patient surveys such as HCAHPS and the upcoming Clinician & Group Consumer Assessment of Healthcare Providers and Systems (CG-CAHPS), coupled with the free anonymous space of social media sites, has created a wealth of patient satisfaction data that can be triangulated and integrated to develop an in-depth characterization of healthcare organizations, hospitals, and individual providers. This surge of data leaves providers more vulnerable to negative information than ever before.

COLLECTING AND ANALYZING ALL SENTIMENTS

Very few tools offer providers a full understanding and increased influence over their online reputations, which can affect current business as well as future reimbursements. Physicians, digital marketers, business executives, and social strategists need a complete spectrum of actionable insights by operational categories to form and execute a social business strategy. At the heart of this strategy is an understanding of the feedback, opinions, emotions, and subjective comments from patients that can form the basis for action to improve business operations and patient experiences. The vast majority of patients have positive experiences with the care they receive from their providers, and given the opportunity, they are more than willing to share positive feedback with their peers. Healthcare providers must seize opportunities to aid patients in sharing positive experiences and opinions with the online community. Simultaneously, they must seize opportunities to examine negative social media feedback to improve their internal processes and services. Transparency and accountability are the norm for physicians and hospitals, and not recognizing this fact can result in further physician disempowerment and vulnerability.

The best approach to extracting the strategic value of social media feedback is to move beyond high-level listening and employ new technology that transforms unstructured, raw data into actionable insights. Zach Hofer-Shall, a leading expert on social media from Forrester Research, writes, "The concept of monitoring social media might sound obvious. Most data-hungry marketers understand the value of their customers' social data. But based on my research, even though most marketers may collect this data, far fewer actually use it to inform an enterprise-view of their customers. As any analytical mind knows: collecting data is only the first step."[2]

Clearly, patient feedback translates to very little useful information without a full understanding of the context, domain, credibility, and topological sentiments of the comments. For example, let's review the following three comments:

- "I loved my experience at Hospital ABC – the doctors were awesome."
- "If the service at Hospital ABC was better, I would have loved it."
- "I loved my visit at Hospital ABC, but it's tough for them to beat out Hospital DEF on location alone."

These comments all address about some aspect of *love* for Hospital ABC, but each has a very different meaning.

The intrinsic approach to arrive at true actionable insight into the previous comments and extract an understanding of the social media unstructured text is by using healthcare-specific neurolinguistic processing (NLP) engines to read, process, and create actionable insights. An effective NLP engine reads through every single mention on the web word-by-word, extracting phrases, themes, key words, anomalies, influence credibility, opportunities, and other aspects of the communication. Additionally, NLP can be combined with credibility assessments for each author and company-specific feedback that converts the social media "feedback fire hose" into well-organized, actionable categorical indicators. The NLP-powered sentiment mining algorithms extract operational intelligence from patient feedback and distill data into actionable insights that can improve subsequent patient experiences across all areas of care.

Figure 3-2: Sample Performance Scorecards from Binary Fountain

CASE STUDIES

The most successful patient-centered organizations understand their patients' perspectives, act upon them, and use them to drive comprehensive operational intelligence throughout their services and organization. Using an unbiased analytic view of patient social media and survey feedback, the following organizations are making business decisions using real-time, unsolicited, and relevant customer feedback to help manage their operational intelligence, online reputation, and patient collaboration. They employ the social business intelligence solution "PatientSI" powered by Binary Fountain, McLean, Virginia.

See Clearly Vision

See Clearly Vision, which operates multiple locations in the highly competitive field of laser eye surgery and ophthalmology, places an extremely strong emphasis on the patient experience. This emphasis has helped them maintain high patient loyalty and obtain actionable insights into areas of improvement. Patient insights are continuously collected with on-site iPads and from online review/recommendation sites using the PatientSI application.

Practice administrators and physicians review patient recommendations, testimonials, survey capture rates, and online ratings and reviews during their monthly staff meetings. Each patient recommendation collected online or via on-site iPad and email is discussed. In response to positive comments, the team reiterates what they're doing well and where they have maintained consistently high marks. When negative comments are made, the team identifies if the comment is justified, and if so, determines what they can do as a group to rectify any issue.

The See Clearly Vision team also recognizes the importance of responding as quickly as possible to a negative review or patient comment. In one example, an unhappy patient posted a negative review on a well-known online recommendation site. Both the practice administrator and the physician received an email alert about the online review. That same day, the practice administrator called the patient to learn more about what had happened and to see what could potentially be done to resolve the issue. The patient was surprised to receive the call and suggested that the practice went above and beyond what was expected simply by calling and listening to what happened. Without being prompted, the patient removed the recent negative comment on the online site.

The team continuously makes both small and large changes to ensure patient comfort during visits. These changes are prompted by suggestions and recommendations taken from the online community and from patients in the office. For example, televisions were installed at each of the practice locations, new magazines were added, and the temperature in the waiting room was lowered, based on patient feedback. Such small changes can often make a big difference.

Since launching the PatientSI application, See Clearly Vision has seen a decrease in the number of negative online reviews and an increase in the number of positive testimonials on various social media and online review sites. Of note, nearly 10% of patients surveyed indicated that they had heard about the practice via online searches (Fig. 3-3). This trend of patients relying on web-based content to choose a provider is expected to continue and even soar in the next several years. Commitment to improving the patient experience can translate into strong patient loyalty and a positive online reputation.

Maryland Oncology Hematology

This large national single-specialty network of nearly 1,000 physicians is constantly striving to gain insight from patients and referring physicians. To that end, the organization has conducted patient surveys for several years using contracted

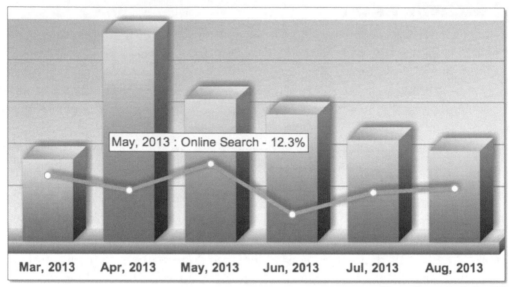

May, 2013 : Online Search - 12.3%

| Mar, 2013 | Apr, 2013 | May, 2013 | Jun, 2013 | Jul, 2013 | Aug, 2013 |

Binary Fountain PatientSI

Figure 3-3. Line chart represents the percentage of patients who heard about the See Clearly Vision practice from online searches.

paper survey systems. Concomitant with these surveys in self-addressed, stamped envelopes, they began providing surveys via an iPad-based medium with PatientSI.

They conducted a direct comparison between these two survey formats with a primary end point of determining the optimal method of obtaining patient experience data. Secondary endpoints included 1) turnaround times, 2) completion rates, 3) ability of the healthcare provider to intervene on data, and 4) physician satisfaction. To provide adequate control for the two survey systems, the same questions were used in both surveys, and both surveys were made available in three office locations: the waiting room, exam rooms, and treatment rooms. Patients could choose either survey method, and each member of the office was informed that regardless of which survey the patient filled out, the department with the most surveys would win an iPad. Data were collected over a 2-month period.

A total of 178 iPad surveys were administered with an average completion rate of 85.5% compared to a total of 37 paper surveys with an average completion rate of 22.5% (Fig 3-4 and Table 3-1). The average turnaround time for the paper surveys was 26 days compared to instantaneous turnaround for the iPad surveys. Physicians could intervene instantly with the iPad survey because a text message or email was sent to the physician when a negative comment was made. For example, one patient had a negative experience with the front desk receptionist and reported her dissatisfaction in the iPad survey, which triggered a text message to the physician. He found the patient before she left the office and intervened to turn the negative experience into a positive one, which she subsequently reported back to her primary care physician.

The two competing survey systems had unique differences in terms of functionality and usability of the data. After collection of the data from the paper surveys, the information was reported back to the physicians several weeks to months later via a paper document coupled with access to an online portal with

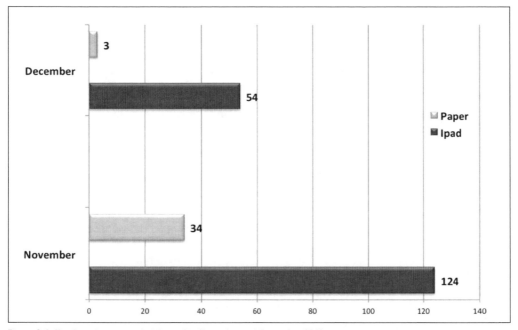

Figure 3-4. Number of surveys administered in November and December 2012.

metrics of the results. These data were used for internal quality assurance within the organization. With the iPad survey, the instantly collected data were presented on a dashboard that was subsequently integrated with all online data that had been collected from the various social media sites to present a composite score about patient experiences. This score was determined by several factors derived from patient comments and grades given to the provider. Such scores allow physicians to track trends in scores over time to ascertain whether implemented improvements actually made a difference in patient experience and satisfaction.

With the consent and permission of the patient, comments made on the iPad surveys or solicited via email could be shared on any of the social media sites,

Survey Type	November	December
Paper	45%	0.03%
iPad	90%	81%

Table 3-1. Survey Completion Rates.

such as Vitals (http://www.vitals.com/), HealthGrades® (http://www.healthgrades.com/), Yelp, Google, Facebook, and Twitter®, to ensure that the physicians' online reputations accurately reflected the opinions of their patients. The patient satisfaction score was substantially greater for the PatientSI survey system than the traditional paper/pencil survey, based on the instantaneous results allowing for rapid intervention.

Johns Hopkins Orthopaedic & Spine Surgery – National Capital Region

Before implementation of a social media monitoring program, one of the primary complaints from patients in this practice was prolonged waiting times in the office. Secondary complaints included issues with parking (parking fees) and lack of responsiveness by the office staff by phone. Several mentions of the wait time in various surveys prompted the office administration to make multiple attempts to alter scheduling templates and reduce the total number of patients seen in clinic sessions. However, such attempts were unsuccessful at solving the patients' perceptions of an excessive wait time.

In April 2012, the practice implemented a real-time, iPad-based, in-office feedback system. Each patient was asked to respond to 23 multiple-choice questions and one free text question regarding the experience in the office for that visit. Several of the questions sought to elicit feedback about the quality of care and attentiveness of the various office staff with whom the patient had contact, including check-in staff, medical assistants, physician assistant, physician, and check-out staff.

The average time for patients to complete the survey was 2 minutes, and the rate of patient response consistently remained in the 50% to 70% range. Initial feedback from the iPad-based surveys suggested that the primary contributors to prolonged wait times were delayed check-in due to missing information (e.g., insurance forms and radiology reports) and excessive time in the examination rooms waiting for the physician assistant, physician, or both. The patients clearly stated that although they were very happy with the quality of non-operative and surgical care from the office and its providers, the wait time was a major contributor to overall dissatisfaction and was perceived as disrespectful to patients and their need to attend to their work and personal schedules. Several patients mentioned that they would not recommend the practice to their family or friends for this reason. Similar responses were posted on social media sites, including HealthGrades® and Vitals. Overall patient satisfaction with the office during initial months using the new feedback system was rated as 2.2 on a 5-point scale.

Based on the feedback, the practice decreased patient load by approximately 20% for 4 weeks, during which time they reorganized the intake process and patient schedule. They gave greater attention to pre-appointment acquisition of reports, insurance information, and new patient forms. The physician and his physician assistant also committed to decreasing the amount of time spent on dictations between patients. After the 4-week phase-in period, the total volume of patients was returned to baseline. The number of complaints about prolonged wait times in the office decreased to 12%. Further, overall patient experience improved from 3.0 to 4.0 in subsequent months. The number of patients stating that they would recommend the practice to family and friends increased from 28 positive comments to 73, and negative posts on online social media sites decreased.

Coincidentally, the number of new patients being referred to the practice increased dramatically, which the physician believes is due, in part, to an improved patient experience resulting from close objective monitoring of patient sentiment. The increase in referrals also could be partly due to new patients reviewing social media ratings and comments about the practice.

Leveraging Social Intelligence

Organizations that dedicate resources to leveraging freely available online feedback can extract a wealth of data about their patients' experiences. The challenge is how best to use the wealth of data to drive marketing and operational strategies.

Effective extraction of the strategic value of social media feedback requires moving beyond high-level listening to using technology that turns unstructured, raw data into actionable insights. Social business intelligence solutions are fundamentally changing how organizations mine credible patient feedback from various online media sources. The results provide decision makers with the actionable insights needed to improve organization operations, patient experience, online reputation, and loyalty that drive bottom-line results.

As Jack Welch, former CEO of General Electric, has been quoted as saying, "An organization's ability to learn, and translate that learning into action rapidly, is the ultimate competitive advantage." Employing an effective social business intelligence platform is the key to translating learning into action.

REFERENCES

1. Brenner J. Pew Internet: Social Networking. Pew Internet and American Life Project. August 5, 2013.

2. http://blogs.forrester.com/zachariah_hofer_shall/10-03-12-what_social_intelligence.

Chapter 4:

Social Media for Healthcare Marketing and Branding

Susan Solomon

TRADITIONAL HEALTHCARE MARKETING

Not long ago, healthcare marketing appeared to be on its last leg. Unimaginative mass media campaigns were the norm, costing millions of dollars with very little return. Healthcare administrators and physicians were frustrated because marketing was an enormous expense, and very few marketers could prove any connection with the healthcare consumer.

Perhaps the most telling send-up of the situation was an entry in "The Weekly Probe," a satirical blog on healthcare marketing, which included a tongue-in-cheek interview with the elderly tandem bicycle-riding couple of stock photography fame who seemed to appear in hospital advertisements across the nation. "They have graced billboards and newspaper ads in the health care world for more than three decades, but have decided to hang up the bike and retire," the piece reads. "Over the 35-plus years since, Steve and Sherry have been photographed on more than 127 different tandem bikes and used in advertising for more than 1,400 hospitals and health systems ... every hospital, system, clinic, doctor or veterinarian could use our photo. And it seemed like they did!" So much for organizations developing unique brands or even considering interacting with their audiences.

One of the most notorious examples of wasteful, and even dangerous, mass healthcare marketing was Merck's promotion of Vioxx® as a superior arthritis medication, despite a lack of evidence that it was any more effective than alternative prescriptions. An estimated 25 million Americans took Vioxx, and Merck made huge profits before discovery of the drug's link to heart problems. That mass advertising campaign, combined with a greater than 80% increase in prescription drug advertising from 1997 to 2005 and smaller-scale but noticeable hikes in marketing by doctors and hospitals, has made the public extremely skeptical of paid messaging from their healthcare providers.

Healthcare marketers cite many reasons for continuing with expensive traditional media vehicles. One of the most popular is that healthcare marketing tends to target seniors, among the last group of newspaper readers and those most effectively reached through traditional advertising. Another reason is anecdotal reports that board members and administrators who were not well-versed in Facebook, Twitter®, or other forms of new media would not support nontraditional advertising plans. Additional reasons include the risk of a potential breach of patient privacy resulting in a HIPAA violation, lack of control over public discussion, uneven quality of information, less obvious return on investment (ROI), and a concern that using social media would be perceived as a tacit acceptance of staff spending time at work on Facebook and Twitter.

Nonetheless, the number of highly successful examples of healthcare marketing via social media is growing. Those who have achieved such success have developed effective precautions against HIPAA violations, used public discussion to the organization's advantage, engaged employees without disrupting their work-lives, and attained meaningful ROI.

NOT GOING BACK TO TRADITIONAL ADVERTISING

Healthcare marketers are scrambling to transition into social media, trying to follow the few pathfinders that have found significant brand-building success by mastering social media strategies. Business leaders know they must go where the customers are, which is why social media makes sense, especially for healthcare marketers looking to increase brand recognition. The essence of branding is to have the key differentiating points about a product or service instantly known by target markets. A familiar tactic is to communicate such differentiating points frequently and with intriguing approaches. Social media, with its deep penetration into daily life as well as its penchant for imaginative message building, is a perfect mechanism for communicating a brand.

Social media also enables a shared community experience at any time of the day that traditional media cannot provide. Additionally, it provides an opportunity to target a specific audience, thus providing better economics for tighter marketing budgets. Finally, consumers are eager for change and expect more from today's healthcare communications and marketing.

The reality is that consumers have been hardwired for getting healthcare information electronically for a very long time. Years before social media demanded their attention, consumers sought health information electronically via early entrants such as Koop.com and, later, WebMD. The natural next step is to disseminate this information via the social spaces.

PHYSICIAN BRANDING AND SOCIAL MEDIA

The use of social media was introduced to physicians very quickly, almost shockingly for many. Just 5 years ago, the thought of a physician asking to be "liked" on Facebook seemed absurd, and asking for a recommendation on Yelp® would have been considered very odd. In fact, Yelp and the rise of online social rating systems propelled most physicians into the social media sphere, often without much support from their hospital's or medical group's marketing departments.

Just as years ago doctors relied on word of mouth to boost their practices, in the new age, they need great ratings on social media platforms combined with a solid plan for managing their online reputation. Accomplishing this task is not always easy, given the search engine dominance of healthgrades® and Vitals in most markets. Entries in these two websites (often with consumer ratings) almost always rise to the top of most online physician searches. Even more disconcerting are the consumer sites that invite consumers to rate doctors alongside local bistros and house painters. Not all of those who comment on these sites are inclined to leave praise.

Just a few years ago, marketing professionals would have advised physicians that simply seeding their websites or bio pages with key search terms was enough to make their self-generated pages rise to the top of the major search engines. However, now it is more complex. Google's Panda, Penguin and Hummingbird programs originally were designed to limit search engine spamming, but the latest updates also penalize many so-called "white hat" search engine tactics, such as adding multiple links or super-optimizing pages. Search engines currently give higher rankings to rich content, including video and participation in social media.

Today's marketers advise physicians to embrace social media, include° tweeting, video, and Facebook pages for their practices. At the very least, a LinkedIn® presence is essential, providing a more serious, professional identity than most other social media sites. Others have made a professional Facebook page to establish an inviting presence in social media.

Kevin Pho, MD, who writes KevinMD.com, the popular blog on physicians and social media, says that his participation in social media not only improves his online reputation but also gives him the confidence of knowing patients are getting good information online. His "ah ha" moment came when he blogged about the Vioxx issues and patients thanked him for his informative, clarifying piece. For others, social media offers the opportunity to provide a more reliable source of healthcare information than Yahoo! Answers, which conspicuously disclaims any responsibility for the accuracy of answers provided by posters.

HEALTHCARE ORGANIZATIONS NEED TO TAKE THE PLUNGE

The time has come for healthcare organizations to move toward greater social media activity. Because social media has pervaded the culture, organizations that are unwilling to join may find both loyal and potential customers engaged elsewhere.

Healthcare, which has an episodic nature, only comes to mind when the consumer needs it. For hospitals that want to interact with most healthy individuals, such a connection is made only when a baby is delivered and then, after a long gap in service, during the senior years. This potentially decades-long gap does nothing to create and support lifetime loyalty. Social media, with its fast and easy connectivity, can create lifelong positive connections outside the episodic, acute-care focus of most hospitals.

Social media also attracts *the engaged patient*, the individual who is sufficiently educated and empowered to participate actively in his or her treatments. Although they sometimes challenge traditional systems, these patients often enthusiastically comply with treatment plans they helped create. They can also be great supporters of healthcare and even more efficient to treat when they actively share in the process of getting better.

HOW TO JUMP IN

Before starting a social media effort, any organization must create a plan that generally boils down to a key strategic question: What do you want to do? The answer could be: build engaged fans (loyalty), capture more business or raise funds (acquisition), engage referral sources (physician relations), or bolster the organization's reputation (branding).

Of note, not all social media works well for every strategy. For example, Facebook builds a brand, but Facebook advertising also can be used for acquisition. Twitter® is great for service recovery. YouTube builds brand and establishes a visual association. Pinterest can target specific segmented interest groups such as young parents. Blogs drive focus toward specific topics for a targeted audience and can be terrific for thought leadership.

Each of these formats requires upkeep that requires more than the services of a college intern. Contrary to popular thought, social media is not free. True effectiveness in the social sphere requires budget. Most healthcare organizations reserve just a small portion of the budget for these efforts, but a few marketing departments have sufficient in-house staff to devote the required time to monitoring of metrics and creation of content. Realistically, organizations must understand that the start-up period requires more resources. Over time, as communications and leaders become more proficient, expenses should decrease.

EXAMPLES FROM HEALTHCARE LEADERS

Almost every hospital in the United States currently is using social media for marketing in some form. Yet, not everyone has a good strategy. The following organizations are clearly strategic in their efforts.

Children's Hospital Boston has discovered how to leverage social media and address almost all of the C-suite trepidation. First, they integrate all their social tools and clearly state what is welcomed and unwelcomed from social media users. Their website is easy to navigate and includes a "Connect with Us" tab that calls out all of the social media tactics they are leveraging, complete with a very straightforward and understandable social media policy that they point out is "in plain English":

"We welcome and encourage open discussion on Children's Hospital Boston's social media sites – including but not limited to our blogs, Facebook,

Twitter, YouTube pages and online story-sharing forums – and look forward to any comments, stories and experiences you want to share.

"That said, we do make reasonable efforts to monitor participation to ensure that you stay on topic, are courteous and avoid making offensive comments. Please remember that information posted on any of our social media platforms shouldn't be considered medical advice and shouldn't replace a consultation with a health care professional.

"Please be aware that once you post something online, there's the potential for thousands (or hundreds of thousands) of people to read your words, even years from now. As a result, we suggest that you exercise caution when posting medical information on any of our social media sites and that you not disclose personal identifiable information like your location, medical record number, financial information, etc."

With the rules of the road established (a longer legal version of the policy also is posted), Children's Hospital Boston can confidently engage people with social media. Their Facebook page (https://www.facebook.com/BostonChildrensHospital) has an enviable 720,000 likes. The wall also has a distinctly branded look and feel, including big pictures of the families the hospital has helped and their intriguing stories. Even more impressive is chatter from fans; more than 100 comments are attached to some of the posts. The content clearly invites engagement.

Children's Hospital Boston's Twitter page (https://twitter.com/BostonChildrens) is branded consistently with their other outlets and frequently updated. It includes lots of news and information on what's happening with the hospital as well as information on fundraising opportunities. A content-rich blog, "Thriving" (http://childrenshospitalblog.org/), is used to dispense pediatric health advice, relay patient stories, and provide a platform for the hospital's doctors and other health care professionals. For example, Dr. Claire McCarthy, a regular contributor, offers both medical and psychosocial commentary, delving into and even calling for an end to the stay-at-home vs. working mom debate.

Onslow Memorial Hospital in Jacksonville, North Carolina, has harnessed the power of blogging – mom blogging to be exact – to target a specific demographic. Set up on platforms developed by the hospital, moms can blog about everything from the best clothes for infants to helping a seriously ill child. With nearly 4 million women with children younger than 18 years blogging, clearly these women have a lot to say. Because women direct most of the healthcare for a family, they surely write about healthcare choices, which makes mom blogging a good tool for healthcare marketers.

Onlsow started with a blog known as Momtalk (http://momtalk.onslow.org/) in 2009. The hospital sought out mom bloggers with a posting on its website, vetted applicants with writing tests and a brief questionnaire, and then let the bloggers have their say (of note, several dads joined in as well). The number of bloggers has grown and in addition to being widely read, many have become local celebrities.

Signature Health Care in Brockton, Massachusetts, also attained success with its mom bloggers. This health system posted a Facebook contest, asking for moms to post the reason why they wanted to be selected. Applicants were asked to have friends and families support or "like" their entries. Eight bloggers were chosen because they met the criteria of being within the health system's service area; showing a sizeable social network; and revealing a positive, wellness-focused attitude.

Both hospitals encourage personal as well as virtual get-togethers for their mom bloggers. Signature (http://signaturemoms.com/) holds regular sessions, giving the bloggers pointers on how to blog, the right length of a blog post, how to invite conversation, and how to use social media tools to ensure that messages "go viral." The bloggers are also encouraged to offer one another support and feedback.

These efforts have a measurable payoff. Onslow's blog has garnered more than 7,000 unique visitors, which the hospital believes has significantly helped raise the hospital's reputation as well as volume for women's health services. In addition, traffic to the hospital's site from the blog has noticeably increased. Finally, the hospital has received substantial positive press since the launch from local papers and *USA Today*.

For service recovery, **Thomas Jefferson University Hospitals** (TJUH) in Philadelphia monitors real-time patient reaction via Twitter (https://twitter.com/TJUHospital). A patient's tweet about a long wait at one of the departments read by the social media department prompts immediate dispatch of a TJUH team member to resolve the issue. The result is better patient satisfaction and avoidance of a backlash of criticisms from other Twitter followers.

St. Joseph Health in Irvine, California, is actively managing the predicament of whether to have staffers outside of marketing join in social messaging. Interested staff complete a social media certification course and subsequently are dubbed "social media chroniclers" for the healthcare system. The course includes extensive lessons in the art of using Facebook (https://www.facebook.com/stjoehealth) and Twitter (https://twitter.com/stjoehealth), including how to engage readers in posts that are widely read and invite conversation. Among the basic information are the importance of posing questions, keeping posts short, and including graphics whenever possible.

Additionally, the social media course includes lessons in the organization's brand "voice," which means use of appropriate words and graphics to convey the brand message. For St. Joseph Health, the brand message is that St. Joseph Health physicians and other caregivers understand that every moment of good health matters. Social media asks engaged audience members about important lifetime events and depicts how the healthcare professionals work to preserve such moments, creating intriguing conversations and extensive participation.

Armed with social media lessons and a good working knowledge of the system's brand, employees push content through the social channels. The greater the amount of such content, the stronger the voice becomes.

Room to Experiment

One of the great assets of social media is the ability to experiment. Facebook does not offer a test environment or any way to simulate campaigns and ads, but the relatively low costs allow for testing. Social media consultants Bright Whistle and **Duke Raleigh Hospital** ran dozens of ads with varied targeting options, ads types, creative content, and landing page destinations. Some of the questions they hoped to answer were: What targeting options are most effective? What drove down campaign costs? What is the difference between using Facebook versus an external landing page (in other words, keep respondents in Facebook or drive to a landing page outside the platform)? All of the Facebook ads generated thousands of data points that were measured and analyzed to help the marketers shape their future ad campaigns. The results documented a 70% increase in campaign efficiency, resulting in 70% lower cost per click and a vast increase in Facebook ad click-through rates. After thoroughly analyzing the data, the team was able to create single posts that generated 121 likes, 24 comments, and 5 appointment requests.

Without careful analysis, the data provided by social media could create information overload. Generally, brand awareness can be measured through impressions or reach on Twitter and shared stories and rankings on Klout (which provides a score for "social influence"). Loyalty can be measured by the number of Facebook friends and Twitter followers. Cost savings can be measured by calculating the cost per click for social media advertising campaigns.

To calculate ROI, providers can track referral sources and integrate these data into customer relationship management systems to achieve a quantifiable impact. Over time, a social media effort should show respectable conversion rates, lowering overall costs of the effort. Eventually, a marketing department should be able to document the savings incurred from substituting social media for traditional advertising.

REFERENCES

1. Famous septuagenarian couple on tandem bike retires from stock photo career. March 30, 2009, http://www.weeklyprobe.com/2009/03/tandem-bike-retires-from-stock-photo-career.

2. Solomon S. Ask the expert: The doctor will Tweet you now – is there a compelling case for physician-directed social media strategy? *eHealthcare Marketing and Trends*. September 2012.

3. Solomon S. Good advice for those tempted to try Facebook ads. *eHealthcare Marketing and Trends*. February 2013.

Chapter 5:

Social Media at a Community Hospital: Rapid Change Requires Rapid Response

Adam Shapourian

The Internet and social media have opened tremendous opportunities to engage individuals faster and with more precise targeting. A plethora of information is readily accessible to consumers. Just a few keystrokes allow a person to ask a wide variety of questions. However, many questions in the healthcare arena cannot be answered with a quick Google search, such as: What is the right medication to take? Is this treatment right for me? How much longer do I have to live?

To research such difficult questions and connect with others who may have similar concerns, consumers may participate in community forums, visit sites such as WebMD® and healthfinder.gov, or use their personal social media accounts. The difficulty is determining whether the information they find is credible. To answer this need, Suburban Hospital has taken an active role in connecting people with the information that can help them take control of their health.

ABOUT SUBURBAN HOSPITAL

Suburban Hospital is a community-based, 236-bed hospital in Bethesda, Maryland. A member of Johns Hopkins Medicine, Suburban Hospital is the designated trauma center for Montgomery County and is located in close proximity to the National Institutes of Health and Walter Reed National Military Medical Center and is only 10 miles from the White House.

Social media has slowly joined the mix of traditional communications tactics at Suburban Hospital. The organization has introduced blogs and various social networks and has invested in social intelligence applications that allow leveraging of social data to measure patients' sentiments and that aid in recruitment efforts.

People now can connect with Suburban Hospital in ways that until recently were simply not available. By hiring staff members who have an understanding of how clinicians interact with patients combined with a familiarity of how technology can improve clinical outcomes and the patient experience, Suburban Hospital has been at the forefront of social media's application in healthcare. They have taken an active role in connecting people with information from credible sources to help them take control of their health.

BUILDING A SOCIAL PRESENCE
160 CHARACTERS AT A TIME

Facebook Use

Approximately 3 years ago, various people within the organization wanted to create individual Facebook accounts for Suburban Hospital. The administration decided to create an organization page (https://www.facebook.com/SuburbanHospital) (Figure 5-1) that was centrally managed by the marketing and communications department, but had no well-conceived strategy for best using social media to engage patients and the community. We quickly realized that sending out a post and hoping it would "stick" was unrealistic.

Figure 5-1. Suburban Hospital's organization page.

Since that initial point, we have been expanding our social presence to increase our audience and branching out to other social networks, such as Twitter® (https://www.twitter.com/suburbanhosp), YouTube (http://www.youtube.com/user/SuburbanHospital), Yelp® (http://www.yelp.com/biz/suburban-hospital-bethesda), and Google+ (https://plus.google.com/+suburbanhospital). Each social network has a unique set of goals and objectives, to which we try to adhere to maintain the integrity of our presence on these networks. Some of the objectives overlap, but individual posts must fit within the overall strategy of the specific social network.

In addition to behavioral health and emergency services, Suburban Hospital maintains specialties in neurosurgery, orthopedics, cardiology, and cancer care. We formed our initial social media strategy around these service lines, providing health information relevant to the patients we serve. Our overall social media strategy is to provide credible health-related information that is localized for our community. Our following will never rival that of the Cleveland Clinic, Mayo Clinic, or even our parent hospital of Johns Hopkins, which have international presence in healthcare, but we take pride in delivering information about medical conditions, treatments and procedures, and the latest health trends and news that is important *to our community.*

As a function of this strategy, we offer an "always listening" approach to customer service to enhance patient satisfaction and provide a vehicle for service recovery. Most importantly, we provide the "human element" in healthcare at a time when providers are fighting harder than ever to maintain their bottom lines. We also have a very active recruitment strategy using social and digital tactics to identify and employ a talented and diverse workforce to provide high-quality care.

We use Facebook to post the latest health news, tips for healthy living, medication recalls, and safety information. We want our community to be informed about recent developments in healthcare so they can take control of their health. This strategy is aligned with our patient- and family-centered care model and is the driving force behind our Facebook strategy. We frequently post photos of our employees and their achievements which repeatedly yield the highest engagement from our followers. In addition, we created a "Recipes for Health" blog on our website with recipes chosen and developed by registered dietitians in the hospital that we routinely also post on Facebook. Blogging, which is often overlooked by larger organizations, is a critical component of our digital strategy that pays substantial dividends in driving web traffic and social engagement.

One of the issues we encountered interacting with people on Facebook is that the demographic the hospital serves is hard to reach using social media. Although the 45- to 54-year age bracket is the fastest growing demographic on both Facebook and Google+,[1] many in our community, particularly those 65 years and older, indicate that they have no reason to be familiar with a hospital's specific medical specialties because they trust their physicians to recommend "the best" hospital for treatment/procedure. Past market research data within our community shows that use of social media has almost a nonexistent impact on the decision process for choosing a hospital. This finding led us to retool our social media strategy to bring it more in line with what we know works: physician marketing.

We created "Ask the Expert" physician interview columns on our website (Figure 5-2) that we also post on our Facebook page. In addition, we offer a monthly physician chat where anyone with a Facebook account can log on to our page and interact in real time with a physician to discuss a current health topic. We have had much success in broadening our reach using this tactic and found it to be a great avenue to market our physicians and provide users with access to easily accessible and credible health information. These physician chats have reached users in more than 40 countries worldwide. Although we may not always directly engage our target audience, families and caregivers of elders in need of answers frequently seek this information on behalf of their relatives or friends. Greater creative attempts to reach this audience can have an important impact on a hospital's approach to social media.

Another key demographic at Suburban Hospital is parents of small children. Our pediatric emergency center treats more than 6,000 children annually, creating a built-in audience that can be targeted on social media. We launched a pediatric emergency page (https://www.facebook.com/SuburbanHospitalPediatrics) that is managed by the medical director of pediatrics (Figure 5-3). The innovative spirit of the pediatrics staff was the driving force in creating this page separate from our organization page, which we could not accomplish for every department. However, having identified a clear need for increasing awareness of our pediatrics department and understanding that social media could serve as a launchpad to this target demographic, we decided to create an individual presence for this medical service. The medical director is responsible for curating content on the page as well as answering any questions from followers. The page offers the community a direct line of communication into the pediatrics department, where parents can ask questions, connect with each other, and learn more about the services we offer.

Suburban Hospital
about a minute ago

If you're 50 or over, you should consider adding colorectal cancer screening to your list of New Year's resolutions. A recent report from the Centers for Disease Control and Prevention (CDC) showed that screening rates aren't where they should be (only one in three people are getting tested), despite the fact that colorectal cancer—cancer of the colon or rectum—is the second leading cause of cancer-related deaths in the United States, killing approximately 50,000 Americans per year. The good news is that it's also one of the most preventable cancers, which is where screening comes in. So what are you waiting for?

Suburban Hospital colorectal surgeon Vivek Patil, MD, explains what to expect when getting a colonoscopy, who's at risk for colon cancer, and what you can do to lower your chances of a cancer diagnosis.

READ: http://goo.gl/YxYsXN

#AskTheExpert #Colon #Cancer

Figure 5-2. "Ask the Expert" columns are posted on Suburban Hospital's website and also on their Facebook page.

Twitter® Use

Because most of our audience uses Twitter to interact with us, we post almost everything related to Suburban Hospital and the healthcare industry on this network (https://twitter.com/SuburbanHosp) (Figure 5-4). The format of Twitter

Figure 5-3. Suburban Hospital launched a pediatric emergency page to highlight the pediatric service.

invites easy-to-digest posts that can be sent out quickly to a large audience. Therefore, we are more "liberal" with the number of posts we make on this social network. We publish posts for the general public and the media and frequently share tweets from health partners and colleagues within our health system to increase awareness of the Johns Hopkins Medicine brand. One of the benefits of using Twitter is the ability to reach more of our target demographic. The fastest growing demographic on Twitter is the 55- to 64-year age bracket,[1] which provides more opportunities to engage and interact with our desired audience.

To increase our reach, we use many of the common healthcare-related hashtags on Twitter, such as #cardiac or #ortho to represent our major service lines as well as #ptsafety, #ehr, and #healthapps to garner retweets and mentions from people on Twitter who are not currently following Suburban Hospital. This approach not only increases the reach of each post, but has helped us build our following on Twitter. Hashtags have become increasingly important in social media as more networks embrace them and users become more comfortable with employing them strategically to achieve their goals. Those who are not using hashtags today should start using them tomorrow.

Healthcare providers on Twitter should set up search lists to monitor posts. The possibilities are endless, but we have established search lists to monitor the phrase "Suburban Hospital" to capture comments from users who have not mentioned "@SuburbanHosp" in their tweet. We have put out many fires (both figurative and literal) discovered with this search mechanism.

We have also set up a search list to identify users who are looking for a doctor in our area to direct them to our physician referral service. Not only can we provide a much needed resource for consumers, but often we can convert users captured on search lists to followers and ambassadors of our brand. Finally, in times of potential crisis, an organization can set up a list to monitor certain keywords and

Figure 5-4. Sample of Twitter posts from Suburban Hospital.

Figure 5-5. Suburban Hospital Google+ post.

phrases associated with the event for continuous monitoring of activity in real time across the web and social media.

Google+ Use

The latest asset in our digital toolset is Google+, which offers specific advantages in the search engine optimization/search engine marketing arena. Google+ posts are tied in with Google search, which has increased the number of impressions in Google searches. Because there is a heavy technology following on this network, most of our posts on Google+ are related to healthcare technology and use hashtags related to this subject, including #hit and #HealthIT (Figure 5-5). Google+ also has health communities with very large and active followings, prompting us to post healthy recipes (#healthyeating, #RecipesforHealth) and tips for healthy living (#healthyliving). Google Hangouts provides the opportunity for people to connect with healthcare experts and learn more about diseases and medical conditions straight from the source.

The popularity of Google+ has been growing slowly and is highly debated, but this network will absolutely become more in the mainstream over the next couple years. Our page has been very slow in gaining followers, but our posts within the health communities have generated a fair amount of +1s, and the content on our page is helping close the loop between search and social.

SOCIAL MEDIA AND THE PATIENT EXPERIENCE

Social media is particularly adept at allowing us to show the "human element" of healthcare. We love interacting with our community and always welcome feedback. We routinely forward positive comments to the supervisor in charge of the unit or department mentioned, but we also value negative comments, which provide us with an opportunity to improve our services and care. The many social media platforms we use provide a very large listening "ear" and additional chances to make a positive impact on the lives of those who we serve. We welcome feedback from our community about their recent experience with the hospital. If they are in need of follow-up communication from our patient relations department, we notify the appropriate staff.

We use some technology to measure patient sentiment, which creates further opportunities for service recovery if a patient has a negative perception of Suburban Hospital. We can monitor Hospital Consumer Assessment of Healthcare Providers and Systems (HCAHPS) data and aggregate Press Ganey survey data into an easy-to-analyze social dashboard. These results directly affect hospital reimbursements and provide high-level insight in this new era of healthcare. By having these data immediately available, the hospital can identify areas of opportunity, enabling us to better implement new processes from the collected feedback. These processes such as improving way-finding and signage, distributing educational materials, and empowering patients to be in control of their care, are important aspects of our patient- and family-centered care model.

Social media has changed only certain aspects of how the hospital processes information and communicates with our audience. The remainder of the patient experience is controlled by the staff interacting with patients on a daily basis. In some cases, the first interaction with the hospital is made on social media. The patient may have read a blog post about a new hospital unit, was looking for a doctor and found our physician referral service, or simply made a comment on Twitter about having a scheduled procedure. In these situations, the social media manager sets the stage and creates expectations for the visit. However, from the moment a patient or family member enters the hospital, he or she has countless interactions with hospital employees from the admissions staff to the nurses and physicians to the transportation and environmental services teams. Opening a direct line of communication to patients or visitors creates an opportunity for service recovery if they have a negative experience and shows these people the proactive efforts being undertaken to improve their experience at the hospital.

Having a hospital staff that understands how patient satisfaction can be affected at every level is extremely important to the culture of the organization and the bottom line.

FINDING EMPLOYEES IS AS EASY AS FINDING FRIENDS

At Suburban Hospital, our recruitment department actively uses technology to meet their mission of maintaining a talented workforce that lives the values of our organization. Reliance on print advertising has decreased in the world of recruitment, and over the past year, our human resources department has focused greater efforts on digital marketing.

In addition to search engine marketing and placing advertisements on job boards such as Indeed® and Monster®, our human resources department is placing ads on Facebook and LinkedIn®. They use social intelligence applications that leverage the power of social media to identify potential candidates for positions across the organization in a passive environment that allows recruiters to spend less time trying to source candidates and more time interviewing and closing the hire.

We have incorporated recruitment tactics into our overall social media strategy to aid in this effort. We frequently post staff achievements on our Facebook page to celebrate the work they do both personally and professionally. We highlight our new hire orientation to create a more interactive process. The staff has created a blog to discuss why they joined Suburban and what has kept them working at our organization for so long. Recruitment campaigns now begin with establishing a digital presence as the priority, building additional elements to support this model.

As a result of this retooled strategy, the human resources department has decreased their spending on traditional advertising by 30% and has shifted funds to innovative new methods of capturing potential candidates. Productivity has increased, but not without hurdles. One of the challenges in adopting this new strategy for recruiting candidates is getting a buy-in from the recruiters. Change is always hard to navigate, especially when dealing with technology, but as the technology becomes more familiar and the team embraces these tools to enhance their skills, the department should be better positioned for the future of recruiting.

ADVICE FOR SOCIAL MEDIA MANAGERS

Although social media itself is a trending topic, it is important to remember that digital and social media represent one component of the larger picture for the hospital. Maintaining a unified message and producing stimulating content is the first priority. Social media is an important vehicle to deliver the message, but it also can expose organizations and make them vulnerable to attack. Every hospital social media manager should be aware of some drawbacks to social media:

Almost everything posted on the Internet is permanent. Choose your words carefully as they could come back to haunt you. Every post should be carefully considered and tied to a specific objective. Don't post a tweet simply to post a tweet. If there is no specific purpose for a post, you run the risk of losing credibility and pushing away your audience.

Don't feed the fishers. Because social media is one of the easiest methods of placing your opinion in front of a mass audience, people who think poorly of your facility and want to make a negative impact on your reputation may tempt you with a tweet or a post designed to illicit an unfavorable response and make the situation worse for your organization. Be smart about what you choose to respond to and consult with your patient relations liaison. There may be additional information about the person making the post of which you are not aware, such as an ongoing dispute over a bill.

Protect patients' privacy. Patient privacy is one risk associated with the use of social media in healthcare that cannot be ignored. Consult your legal counsel and HIPAA privacy office before developing your social media strategy. Although use of Facebook and Twitter is free, the cost of a HIPAA violation while using these social networks could be huge.

CONCLUSION

As we prepare for the next era of delivering healthcare, we will continue to look for more ways for technology and social media to assist us in patient education, patient satisfaction, recruitment, and much more. With increasing numbers of people joining the social media revolution, the generation gap in using these tools should decrease, offering even more opportunities for healthcare facilities to engage their audiences. Organizations that do not embrace this technology will be left behind and eventually flat line.

REFERENCE

1. *Stream Social Quarterly Social Platforms Update. Q1 – 2013.* GlobalWebIndex Blog/Post. https://www.globalwebindex.net/Stream-Social. Accessed November 19, 2013.

Disclaimer: *The views and opinions expressed on Suburban Hospital social media sites and links to other Internet platform sites do not necessarily represent those of Suburban Hospital or Johns Hopkins Medicine. We cannot be held responsible for the accuracy or reliability of information posted by external parties. While Suburban Hospital makes reasonable efforts to monitor and moderate content posted on its social media platforms, Suburban Hospital does not moderate all comments at all times and may not respond immediately to online requests.*

Chapter 6:

Intermountain Healthcare's Intermountain Moms Campaign

Craig Kartchner, Marketing Director, Intermountain Healthcare

SOCIAL MEDIA AT INTERMOUNTAIN

Demographics about the system which comprises Intermountain Healthcare is best presented using the infographic below.

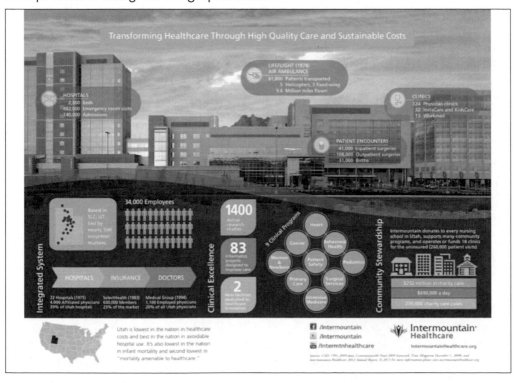

In many respects, Intermountain Healthcare has been conservative since its inception as a community donation of 15 hospitals from The Church of Jesus Christ of Latter-day Saints in 1975. Now it includes 22 hospitals, more than 185 clinics, and 1,100 employed physicians. Despite its conservative past, it is a very forward-thinking organization. For example, Intermountain's research teams and medical informatics systems have shaped how data-driven healthcare is delivered. Clinical experts have created evidence-based best practice protocols that have been adopted by other healthcare organizations. The combined conservatism and innovation was in evidence when the communications department began using social media to communicate with the public.

Just as Utah was part of the "Wild West of the American frontier," the social media arena in 2008 offered no barrier to entry, which resulted in nearly every doctor, nurse, clinic, and service line starting a Facebook page. Hospitals, physicians, and clinics clamored for a presence on social channels that, once developed, were never actually used. The following on these social pages generally consisted only of other staff members and their families, not the target demographic. Intermountain had no central strategy to guide the number or type of posts, promotions, live chats, monitoring, integration with websites, or any other communications function. The result was "each clinic for itself," with little value delivered to end users.

The organization needed an immediate plan to organize these different social channels. The goal was to generate followings and meaningful interactions by using two of Intermountain's greatest resources: its experts (more than 1,000 physicians and 8,400 nurses) and content (thousands of existing patient education materials). The result is a centrally developed, system-wide group of social channels organized primarily by service line that seeks organic growth through actionable content and focuses on meaningful engagement. Nine clinical programs govern clinical quality initiatives and ensure that they are aligned with the best practice protocols: cardiac, cancer, primary care, intensive medicine, pediatrics, women and newborns, patient safety, behavioral health, and surgical services. This structure provides a logical approach to organizing social channels and content.

THE START OF INTERMOUNTAIN MOMS

Intermountain's first strategic foray into the social media realm was in the women and newborn service line. This clinical area was chosen for seven reasons:

1. Target Demographic: The target demographic (women in their childbearing years, with an emphasis on first-time moms) is very active on social channels.

2. Experts: Intermountain Healthcare has clinical experts in a wide variety of specialties and subspecialties in this area.

3. Happy Event: Pregnancy, labor and delivery, and childrearing are generally happy events that people are eager to discuss and share with others.

4. Gateway Experience: Women frequently are the healthcare decision makers in the home. Their first major healthcare decision is often where to deliver their first child and which doctor to ask to help. Providing a positive experience

in the clinics and hospitals during this experience offers a greater chance of capturing patient loyalty and business for future healthcare needs.

5. Highly Engaged in Care: Women in this target demographic are often highly motivated to be engaged in their care and the care of their children. They seek information and interaction with caregivers and other moms.

6. Audience Open to Recommendation: In our experience, women in this target audience are responsive to recommendations from friends, family, and trusted caregivers. Social channels can be an excellent avenue to provide these recommendations.

7. Good Communications Opportunity: Social media may offer some of the best approaches to encourage interaction between moms, clinicians, and other moms.

"Intermountain Moms" was an integrated campaign that included television, radio, print (Fig. 6-1), outdoor, and online promotion, but it focused on social

Figure 6-1. Intermountain Moms magazine advertisement.

channels as the "call to action" rather than traditional web. This campaign represented the first sizable dedication of marketing resources to social channels.

CAMPAIGN GOALS

The goal of the campaign was to engender loyalty throughout the "gateway" healthcare experience by becoming the trusted resource for quality, credible, frequent education. A more specific goal was to provide a convenient forum for women to interact with Intermountain clinicians and other new moms. Not only would such interaction create lasting relationships and introduce women to other clinical areas, but it would ostensibly increase clinical quality and decrease costs as women obtained necessary information to influence their healthcare decisions positively.

BUILDING AN AUDIENCE

Measuring the efficacy of social campaigns through a quantifiable metric, particularly in the healthcare industry, can be difficult. What is the worth of a "like" on Facebook? Our initial drive was to quickly increase likes on the Intermountain Moms Facebook channel (https://www.facebook.com/intermountainmoms), but such numbers are not meaningful without interaction between the target audience and clinicians. Nonetheless, we needed an audience with whom our clinicians could interact. We neither could nor wanted to compete with larger healthcare content sites, but we had an opportunity to become the trusted engagement leaders with our local demographic.

For those reasons, we focused on building an audience on the channel through:

1. Organic growth via excellent educational content
2. Paid promotions: contests/giveaways, collateral distribution, face-to-face communications between clinicians and patients, Facebook ads

Figure 6-2. Intermountain Moms Facebook page.

To build an audience quickly and generate meaningful engagement, we executed several tactics soon after launching the page (Figs. 6-2 and 6-3):

- Video Q&A and video biographies of clinical experts
- Video tours of labor and delivery units throughout the Intermountain system
- Live chats with clinical experts at least weekly in physicians' offices throughout the Intermountain system
- Physician and facility finder tools
- Baby announcer app that allows users to select from several dozen templates and color palettes to design a custom announcement and send it to friends and family via email or social channels (Fig. 6-4)
- Baby photo of the day, in which users were asked to send photos of their babies to use on the Facebook canvas. The daily changing banner pictures spurred growth because friends and family shared the page. Likes grew quickly. To this day, the Intermountain Moms profile icon says "Baby Photo of the Day" (Fig 6-5).
- Nurse Dani, who represents the face of Intermountain Moms (Fig 6-6). Labor and Delivery registered nurse Danielle Kurtz, "Nurse Dani," provides weekly live chats, films dozens of answers to questions posted on the page, and goes to community health events. She has become a trusted source for regular, reliable clinical information. As a local celebrity, she is mentioned constantly in online conversations and is recognized in local grocery stores and malls.

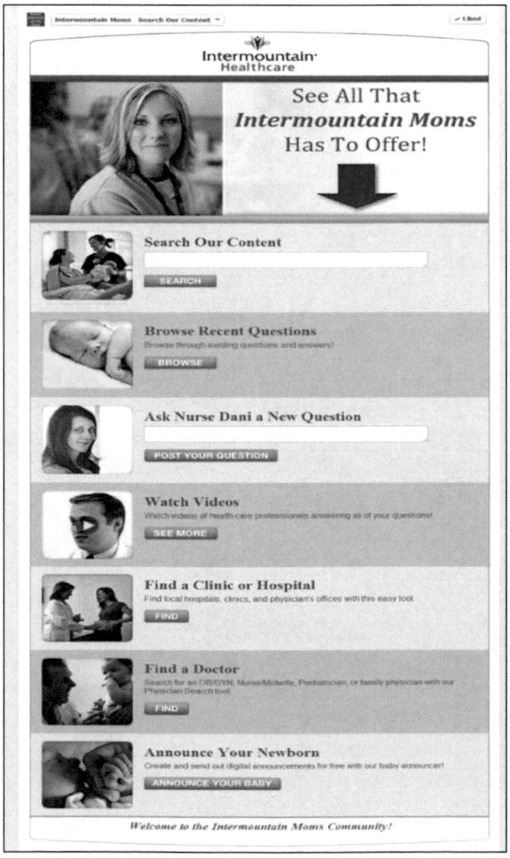

Intermountain Moms has developed a substantial library of educational content. Users can ask questions on the page or search the content library to see if their question has already been answered. Users can also find video tours of all Intermountain labor and delivery areas, biographical videos of hundreds of physicians, and many other educational pieces.

We were initially very concerned about responding to specific questions on Intermountain Moms. Would we be liable if adverse events occurred? Would users defer to Dani's content over their physician's? Would women watch Intermountain Moms videos in lieu of medical appointments? After discussions with the legal department, we carefully instructed all clinicians who interact with the public on Intermountain Moms to provide NO

Figure 6-3. Contents of the online community.

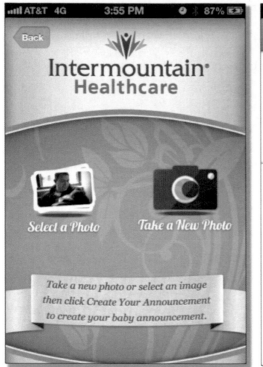
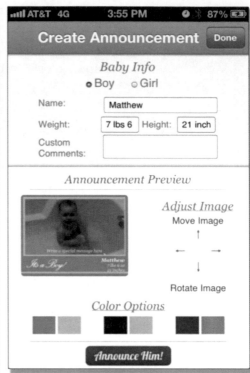

Figure 6-4. Baby announcer app.

Figure 6-5. Baby photo of the day.

diagnoses, prognoses, or any other specific medical advice. We scripted language in the vein of, "generally women with _____ condition experience _____ or _____, but you should consult your personal medical professional about your particular case." The marketing and legal departments carefully and regularly

Figure 6-6. Nurse Dani.

monitor the page to ensure that specific medical advice is not given. The intent of the page is to provide general education and encourage women to develop meaningful relationships with their physicians for detailed, specific information.

PROMOTION

The primary promotion strategy was to have caregivers promote the page directly to the target audience. Women appear to have greater trust in a recommendation from doctors or nurses than in information from a Facebook ad. We created posters and rack cards for physicians' offices, flyers for labor and delivery admission packets, inserts for billing statements, and communications from our insurance division. Although effective, these materials pale in comparison with direct word-of-mouth promotion from trusted caregivers.

INVOLVING PHYSICIANS

Physicians and, to a lesser extent, mid-level providers, did not initially see the value of Intermountain Moms, making it difficult to convince them to take time to participate in video sessions. They did not understand the value of a live chat, which we try to host on the page at least once a week. One of the biggest indicators that the campaign's success, therefore, is the number of clinicians who now request to be on Intermountain Moms. Many of these physicians indicate that patients, staff, and friends had commented on a "cool new campaign called Intermountain Moms" that they had seen in the social world. Several physicians learned they could trust the content and the delivery mechanism as an effective method of sharing clinically accurate information with patients and became comfortable supporting the sites and sending their patients there. As Libby Kelly, MD, stated: "Social networking has clearly become a more important part of what I do professionally. I believe social channels are a great way to educate the public on important issues that affect their health. I have connected with hundreds of people through social channels like Intermountain Moms, and I hope the information I've disseminated has been valuable. Furthermore, I have gained patients from time invested on social channels."

STARK LAW CONSIDERATION

Intermountain Healthcare is a mixed-model system that employs approximately 1,000 physicians, with another 4,000 physicians having privileges in the hospitals at various levels of affiliation. Federal Stark laws relating to physician referrals prohibit Intermountain from spending marketing dollars to promote physicians that it does not employ. However, independent physicians wanted to be on Intermountain Moms, and hospital administrators wanted to keep these physicians happy and not lose their admissions. Because the legal department concluded that the Q&A videos and live chats on Intermountain Moms represented marketing, only Intermountain-employed physicians could participate. As a compromise, all credentialed medical staff physicians are listed in the physician search. Neither employed physicians and their managers nor affiliated physicians and hospital administrators are completely satisfied with this solution, but the solution offers a quiet détente.

EXPANSION

Great content and a wealth of qualified experts build an audience, but giveaways represent a major attraction, which led to the development of the "Daily Delivery." By clicking on a tab on the Facebook page, entrants can fill out a form and be considered for a daily prize. To attract the target demographic, giveaways are items that are bought in large quantities in the labor and delivery units, such as diapers, formula, and bottles. To qualify for the prizes, participants must interact with Intermountain Moms by sharing our posts, recommending us to friends, or posting photos to our timeline.

The response to the Daily Delivery has been enormously positive, with a rapid growth of likes and skyrocketing numbers of interactions. Users "suggested" us to friends on Facebook, reposted our content, tagged Nurse Dani, and posted about Intermountain Moms on their walls. By early 2012, 6 months after its launch, the Intermountain Moms Facebook page had 5,000 likers.

GOING MOBILE

The growth of mobile devices, specifically smart phones, is hard to ignore. Proud parents no longer bring their laptops to the delivery room to email friends and post pictures on social channels. In fact, many parents do not even bring cameras other

than the ones on their phones. To meet their needs, Intermountain Moms now has a mobile app called "Baby Steps." It started as an announcement app with dozens of stylized announcement templates and has expanded to include tools such as an immunization tracker,

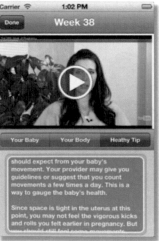

Figure 6-7. Baby Steps phone app.

week-by-week pregnancy updates and health tips from Nurse Dani, a baby name generator, a countdown clock, a video library, a pregnancy diary, and more (Fig. 6-7). For many, this free app is their introduction to Intermountain Moms.

ADDING PEDIATRICS

Pediatric content on Intermountain Moms initially was limited, but many of the questions and comments on the channels were related to pediatrics. In response to these queries, we have videotaped pediatricians and others on such pediatric topics as summer safety, allergies, asthma, car seats, helmets, attention-deficit/hyperactivity disorder, autism, and immunizations. Pediatric specialists from various Intermountain Healthcare facilities conduct live chats, and pediatric questions are sent to specialists for qualified responses.

We also added pediatric content and tools to the Baby Steps mobile app (Fig. 6-8). The app now features Nurse Dani describing important developmental milestones in children's early lives. In contrast to pregnancy videos that address weekly developments throughout gestation, the pediatric videos are organized according to other logical dates, such as 1 month, 6 months, 1 year, and 2 years.

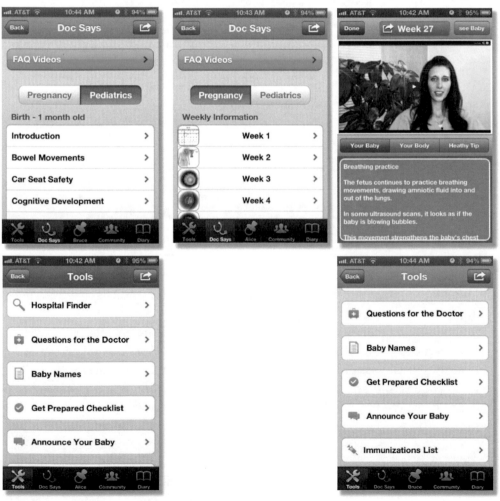

Figure 6-8. Comparison of pediatric and pregnancy mobile phone apps.

The recently launched immunization calendar on Baby Steps (Fig. 6-9) provides an easy method to track all the immunizations for a family. The calendar contains color-coded charts that indicate all the required vaccines children should receive and provides push notification reminders for when the vaccinations are due.

Although we host virtually all Intermountain Moms videos on YouTube, advertising on this site is not currently a large part of our media mix. Presently we are working on a series of pre-roll and Trueview ads to promote Intermountain Moms. We also are planning a campaign with several dozen YouTube celebrities to talk about Intermountain Moms on their channels and push people to interact with Intermountain caregivers. Recognizing that YouTube is the world's second-largest search engine, we are carefully analyzing video metadata to achieve the best results.

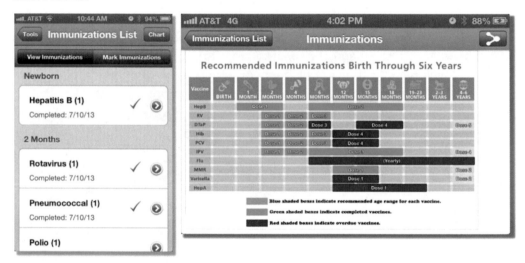

Figure 6-9. Immunization mobile phone apps.

THE RISE OF OTHER SOCIAL MEDIA

The growth of other social media, such as Instagram, Pinterest, Twitter, and Vine, expands our ability to connect with women in our target audience. In fact, these channels skew toward our target audience of women in their childbearing years. Pinterest and Instagram are highly image-centric, which lends itself well to the joys of having and raising children.

As we create Intermountain Moms profiles on other social channels, we heavily cross-promote with Facebook, our websites, and other properties. With every "Photo of the Day Submission," for example, we request permission to share the photo on our Pinterest and Instagram channels. We also link Facebook posts to relevant posts on the Intermountain blog network (http://intermountainhealthcare.org/blogs/pages/home.aspx?category=Intermountain%20Moms), connect tweets to Facebook posts, and connect Pinterest posts to Facebook posts.

We also have recruited another important influencer for our target audience: so-called mommy bloggers. We invited a dozen local bloggers to meet Nurse Dani and take a tour of the Facebook page and newly launched mobile app. Many reported previous positive experiences with Intermountain Healthcare, and all responded positively to the campaign's goal of educating women and providing resources to aid in child-bearing and -rearing. These bloggers wrote about Intermountain Moms, promoted the channels, and responded to questions and comments.

We also participate in a variety of local health fairs and events, some sponsored by Intermountain Healthcare and some independent. Nurse Dani typically headlines our space at these events, meeting women and answering questions in person and online.

Dani is featured in a variety of television and radio interviews, primarily through existing Intermountain Healthcare media partnerships (Fig. 6-10). She has become a popular guest because of interest in the content she offers and her engaging personality. Several media outlets have requested additional interviews beyond partnership obligations.

Figure 6-10. Nurse Dani on a local television show.

One media partnership that paid particular dividends in late 2012 was Baby Your Baby, a collaboration between the Utah State Department of Health, Intermountain Healthcare, the local CBS affiliate, and a group of radio stations. The program prepares women for pregnancy, labor and delivery, and raising children through education and better access to care. Because Intermountain Healthcare had already developed the social channels, education content, and other features of Intermountain Moms, the Baby Your Baby committee agreed to make Intermountain Moms the official social channels of the Baby Your Baby campaign. The Baby Your Baby website (http://babyyourbaby.org/) points to the Intermountain Moms Facebook page, as do all of the partners' social channels relating to Baby Your Baby.

By early 2013 our Facebook page had more than 21,000 likers, and thousands had started to follow our Pinterest boards, tweets, and blog posts. The Intermountain Moms social channels are Intermountain Healthcare's fastest growing and most successful social property in terms of likers, interactions, and educational content produced.

THE NEXT FRONTIER: PATIENT ENGAGEMENT

One of the most important endeavors underway at Intermountain is patient engagement, defined as involving patients in the healthcare team and giving them a voice in their own care. As Channing Thomas, a Salt Lake City mom stated: "Intermountain Moms has helped me with Nurse Dani answering my questions. I have asked questions about my son and about trying to get pregnant again. I love the articles they post about parenting information. It's just nice to have a page like Intermountain Moms to go to with questions."

Patient engagement efforts can be described as any tool, education, or activity that enables patients to interact meaningfully with caregivers and become more accountable for their own health. Intermountain Moms has enormous potential to be precisely that tool and to connect women with providers. The next phase of Intermountain Moms and all Intermountain Healthcare patient communications will have elements of patient engagement. The success of Intermountain Moms will be judged by whether we can positively influence patient behavior through education and more regular communication with caregivers. Our approach includes targeted emails and texts, push notifications, gamification (use of game thinking and game mechanics in non-game contexts to engage users in solving problems) on social channels, personalized web experiences, and interactions using our patient portal.

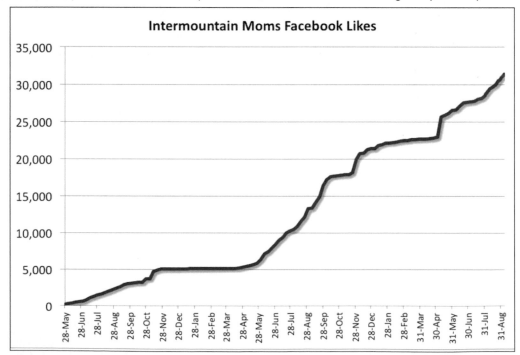

Figure 6-11. Growth of Intermountain Moms Facebook likes.

Intermountain Moms will be the proving grounds for broader patient engagement strategies.

SUCCESSES AND LESSONS LEARNED

As the time of this writing, Intermountain Moms has more than 30,000 likers (Fig. 6-11), and its average reach is more than 200,000 each week. Measured simply by number of followers, the Intermountain Moms campaign is the largest and fastest growing social community at Intermountain Healthcare, but it pales in comparison to communities of some other health systems. Perhaps its success can be measured better in terms of meaningful interactions on its sites: the questions asked and answered, the easier access to valuable education, the improved health and lives, and the clinician's job made easier by offering a credible source of information for patients.

Even more importantly, the campaign promises to be an integral part of Intermountain's patient engagement efforts. Tools developed for the Intermountain Moms campaign can be applied to many service lines and clinics, and very specific audiences can be targeted to better connect with caregivers. Intermountain Moms helps make patients and community members active members of their healthcare teams and serves as a model for other clinical areas.

Chapter 7:

Children's Online Social Network: Building on Patient Ideas

Amanda Biegler Wall

I am in a meeting discussing the organization's online tools for patients and families. Someone asks about support group information, noting that specific patient populations commonly are interested in connecting with both physical and virtual support groups. I reply, "Yes, of course we can link to information about patient and family support groups. However, you should know that Children's has an online private social network. Children's Patient and Family Social Network is a virtual network similar to Facebook. Patients and their families use it as an online support group. The Patient and Family Social Network allows families to create a profile and connect to other families by joining communities." The person responds, "Wow! I didn't know we had that. Is that safe? What if they say something bad about us?" I inform them that the site is not monitored, but families can report other users. Conversations of this type remain common, almost 3 years after the site was launched.

ABOUT CHILDREN'S MEDICAL CENTER DALLAS

Children's Medical Center has provided healthcare for children for more than a century. It is the only academic healthcare facility in north Texas dedicated to the comprehensive care of children from birth to age 18 years.[1,2] Patient care ranges from standard eye examinations to specialized treatment in heart disease, hematology-oncology, and cystic fibrosis. Children's also is a major pediatric kidney, liver, heart, and bone marrow transplant center. In 2006, Children's performed the first successful pediatric intestinal transplant and combined heart-liver transplant in north Texas.

This private, not-for-profit medical center is the fifth-largest pediatric healthcare provider in the United States. Children's is the primary pediatric teaching facility for The University of Texas Southwestern Medical Center. Research has focused on developing treatments, therapies, and greater understanding of pediatric diseases.

WHY BUILD A SOCIAL NETWORK?

Healthcare is changing from the doctor telling the patient what to do to a partnership between doctor and patient. Patients and families evaluate the doctor's directions and determine the best course of action for themselves through research and communication. For example, some families investigate herbal and diet solutions instead of or in addition to prescription drugs. Often they seek information from other families. Through such communication, families can either validate their ideas or raise questions about their beliefs and thoughts. To meet this changing healthcare dynamic, Children's is working to provide families with a safe and secure place to gain support, find information, and exchange ideas.

The idea to build a private social network for patients and families of patients at Children's was first proposed by families who received care at the institution. One very instrumental family, who has a little girl with a very rare disorder, approached us after they had little success finding an online network for support. They found a foundation that was willing to help sponsor the launch of a social networking site if Children's would support the tool long-term. The staff at Children's considered this a great opportunity to meet the needs of patients and parents trying to understand their child's diagnosis and offer support for children with complex conditions. Children's decided to move forward in partnership and collaboration with the family.

The concept and design of Children's Patient and Family Social Network (CSN) (http://www.childrens.com /social-network) started with a major advantage: working in partnership with families. Both patients and their parents seek online support for various medical conditions, but each group has unique needs. We understood that any social network we developed must be different, easy to use, and personalized to offer true value.

OUR FAMILIES' REQUIREMENTS

The first step in design sessions was to determine requirements. Families requested a tool where patients could have a profile, connect with others, and develop a forum for communication and the exchange of ideas. They also wanted a safe environment for their children to find support within a network of others who could share similar experiences.

In discussions about privacy and security, one question recurred frequently: "What happens if someone posts something inappropriate?" The families believed strongly that users of an online network should be able to express themselves freely, without the fear of being monitored, but a balance was required between protecting patients and allowing freedom of expression. If families were required to submit every comment for institutional review before posting, they would feel extremely controlled, and Children's did not have the staff to offer such support over the long term. As with most social networking tools, complete control of the site and its content was unrealistic. Both the strength and the vulnerability of social networking sites is that users generate and maintain the content.

Generally, humans monitor one another in a social environment. For example, if one person at a dinner party monopolized conversation, making loud and outlandish comments, the group likely would change the direction of the conversation, excluding the one person. If the person continued, dinner companions would finish their meals, move away to talk to others, and eventually leave the person without an audience. The same is true of an online community. Users naturally push away from ridiculous comments, and if necessary, report the user. Following this logic, Children's decided to rely on users to self-monitor the site, affording them the ability to create private groups and report other users. Children's responsibility is to respond appropriately to users and comments that are reported to us.

Many patients and families at Children's have created login profiles to view their electronic medical records (EMRs) online. Prior to 2011, to receive a login, families were required to be at the hospital in person to sign a consent form. The logical step for CSN was to use that same login to validate users as patients and families of Children's during registration. Accordingly, we moved registration for online EMR access to an online process, inviting users to join CSN at the same time. The patient's name, date of birth, and EMR number are validated against the EMR system. An automatic prompt offers users the opportunity to join CSN when they sign up to receive their EMRs.

THE TECHNOLOGY

The family who had presented the social network project had a vendor with whom they were interested in working. During conversations with the vendor, two primary needs were determined for the network: 1) Integrating the network with other patient and family online tools including the online EMR, and 2) Supporting the technology long term. Acknowledging these needs, we began to look for other vendors that more heavily integrated with our current technology platform. CSN was one of the first projects to bring the operations, public relations, and information technology departments at Children's together to examine all institutional online projects and determine how to use the technology most effectively.

A social collaboration tool available within a technology partner's product suite was designed to allow employees to network and collaborate. We modified the tool's language to make it family-friendly, concentrating on changing only that which was necessary, primarily content and ease-of-use features. For example, we changed the software feed that said *What are you working on?* to a *Bulletin Board*, modifying the profile questions to be about the patient's experience and diagnoses. We decided to only change necessary items so as to incorporate newer versions of the social collaboration tool with minimal effort.

We also chose this software because of the extensive existing setup. The number of options was almost overwhelming initially. The social collaboration tool included *Feeds, Blogs, Communities, Profiles, Activities, Files,* and subscription features. By purchasing a program within the technology partner's product suite, upgrades would be offered frequently and support would be available if needed.

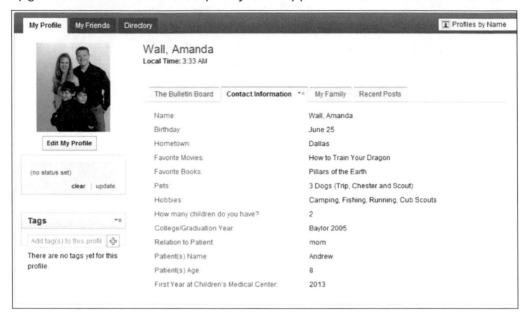

THE RESULTING SOLUTION

Users who log in to childrens.com can view EMR information, message their care team, see patient education, and complete forms or medical self-monitoring tools. The content is tailored to the patient's specific interaction with Children's and the departments the patient or family have visited. For example, the dashboard for those who have diabetes includes an extra navigation item for *Resources* that shows educational tools, a physician blog, and other content specifically for a patient of the endocrinology department.

In the utility navigation, the patient can access CSN. The home page shows a summary of the most recent activities in CSN, and the user can navigate to *Profile*, *Communities,* or other activities. The social network has two environments: one for users 13 to 17 years of age and one for those 18 years and older (Fig. 7-1).

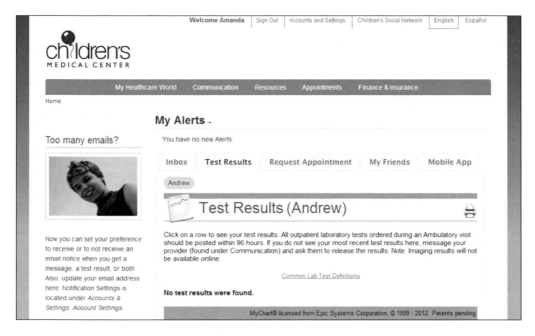

To allow patients to communicate in a safe environment and feel free to express themselves apart from their parents or children, the information shared in each environment is secure and private.

Profile fields are customized to the two age groups. For example, the 13- to 17-year-old environment includes *School* and *Diagnosis*. The user who is 18 years and older is asked for information about both him- or herself and the child who is the patient. Once a patient celebrates his or her 18th birthday, he or she no longer has access to the 13- to 17-year-old environment and is transitioned to the 18 years and older environment. The child's parents are unable to access the patient's EMR information at this point.

Users can navigate to *Communities* to connect with others. Existing communities correlate with clinical department's patient population to give new users easy access to communities of interest to them. Inside a community a user has a blog, forum, feeds, wikis, and bookmarks. Users can meet people who share diagnoses or other attributes within the community and can

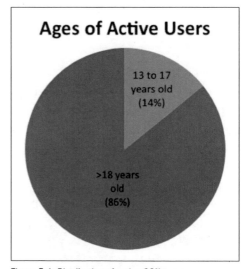

Figure 7-1. Distribution of active CSN users.

create their own communities, setting security based on the level of access they wish others to have.

Users can search for a *Community* via an existing keyword cluster or a customized dropdown list. The dropdown list contains most of the patient populations at Children's and when selected, allows users to see all related *Communities*. For example, clicking on Cancer and Blood Disorders reveals all communities related to cancer. Users who create a new community are required to tag the community with one item in the dropdown list. The consistent keyword list allows the community to be searched for via the dropdown tool, but the user can type in additional keywords.

Based on information provided by users, CSN can recommend connections. In addition to joining a community related to their diagnosis, families connect by experience. Many families go to Camp John Marc, a camp specifically designed for those who have chronic illness or physical disability, and they can connect with other campers via CSN. If two users included Camp John Marc in their profiles, the site might recommend that they befriend one another.

Children's staff can only create an account to either respond to the *Report a User* feature in a technical back-end role or as a patient or family member themself. We developed *Terms and Conditions of Use* specific to social networking and are working on a comprehensive *Terms and Conditions of Use* for the entire childrens.com website, encompassing the public site, portals, the donation site, and CSN. A single *Terms and Conditions of Use* document can ensure that any user at any point on our site can easily connect to the *Terms and Conditions of Use* via the footer on childrens.com.

Our hope is that the CSN site is sufficiently intuitive for families to teach themselves how to use it. However, the technology software offers some help tools. Collapsible content at the top of each section explains the main features. An introductory how-to section walks a user through common questions. For example, if a user selects *I want to upload pictures*, the site says *Try Files*, which hyperlinks to the files section and has a brief explanation of its capabilities.

LESSONS LEARNED

Timing was one of the important factors in establishing CSN. After an initial piloting of the network with a small group of patients and families, we extended the pilot period as we awaited the remainder of the patient portal features to go live. Eventually, we launched CSN and 6 months later re-launched the site integrated with the institutional patient portal. The close development of the two online projects was fortunate. Had they been separated by a year or more, the re-launch of CSN would have been more difficult and created a disjointed experience for users.

The biggest challenge has been user adoption. When a social networking site has little new activity, users quickly lose interest in returning to it. Users are added gradually to all sites. With a healthcare facility social network in which users join a community by patient population, users may feel isolated if others with similar diagnoses have not joined. Finding others by each population type is limited by volume. For example, if only two patients from rheumatology join, they only have each other in that community, despite the entire site having a population of several hundred.

We have built out over eight care team blogs, available on the authenticated patient portal. The care team blogs allow physicians and clinical staff to communicate and present content they want patients and families to read. Thus, Children's can share a clinical perspective with each patient population without staff on CSN. With increased usage of the institution's patient portal, we anticipate increased usage of CSN. However, without staff on CSN, no one is available to add new content, giving patients and families no reason to return to the site. We must discover methods of engaging patients with new content without patients and families feeling monitored.

Staff fears and staff bandwidth have narrowed communication to families and, thus, limited user adoption. Children's has created fliers, table tents, mailers, and integrated notification of patient registration status into the EMR. Mailers had little impact, but quickly identifying an active patient from an inactive patient in the EMR is helpful. If a patient is called out as *Inactive*, a staff member can click on the *Inactive* hyperlink and print a letter, encouraging the patient to sign-up. The letters encourage sign-up for both EMR access and CSN access. Even with the option, however, metrics indicate that only about 50% of staff members are printing letters.

The most successful departments are those in which the physicians are reinforcing the need to sign up online (Fig. 7-2). Patients and families pay more attention if members of the care team go beyond handing patients a flier about CSN, but instead take time to explain the benefits and available features. Families are more likely to remember when a care team member says, "I am happy to refill your prescription today, but in the future you can also do this online." To accomplish

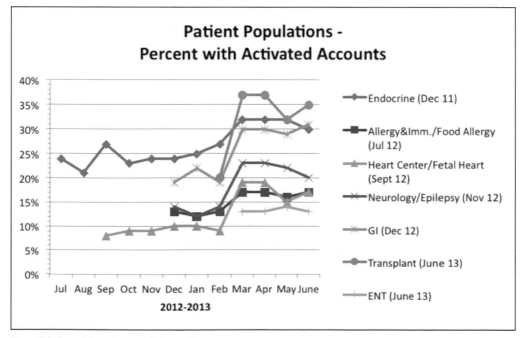

Figure 7-2. Growth in patient populations online.

the goal of greater education about online activities, the care team must be familiar with available features. Unless staff members have a child who has an account, they generally are not informed about the sites. Therefore, we frequently do "road shows" to educate and empower the staff. One staff physician tells his families that they should expect to receive lab results online and will receive a call from the care team only if needed. Online registration in this department is much higher than others.

FUTURE DEVELOPMENT

A social networking platform allows families to find support among each other, but they may need direction on how to console and guide other families in crisis. A training program could result in family volunteers who are accessible for other families. In addition to finding support groups via the care team or searching online, CSN provides a great means for secure connection and support online.

CSN is not just for family support, and can also be used to connect patients who are going through physical and mental stress. Some who have extended hospitalizations may be able to connect both online and in person if they find others in the hospital via CSN. According to one patient who uses CSN, "It's kinda cool to realize that I'm not alone doing this; there's other people out there that can help me."

In addition to establishing CSN as a strong support network among patients and families, we would like to continue to make childrens.com a tailored experience for each audience online, targeting content and tools appropriately. With this approach, we can integrate social media feeds from our public Facebook page (https://www.facebook.com/ChildrensMedicalCenter), Twitter (https://twitter.com/ChildrensTheOne), and our blog (http://blog.childrens.com/) so families can see updates from public social media and CSN presented together. Such integration can drive users to one comprehensive experience.

We continue to investigate innovative methods of incorporating social media into healthcare and meet the needs of our patients and families. Children's mission is "To make life better for children." Through innovations like CSN, we offer patients and their families tools to manage their healthcare better and improve the life of a child.

In remembrance of Judith Kaplan-Einstein, who dedicated herself to seeing Children's Patient and Family Social Network come to fruition.

REFERENCES

1. Children's Medical Center. *Key Facts About Children's: Fiscal Year 2012 (Jan. 1 - Dec. 31).* 2013. http://library.constantcontact.com/download/get/file/1107604773949-327/2012 +Fact+Sheet.pdf. Accessed June 16, 2013.

2. Children's Medical Center. *About Children's Medical Center.* http://www.childrens.com/about-us. Accessed June 16, 2013.

Chapter 8:

Midwives and Marijuana: How the Arizona Department of Health Services Uses Social Media to Build Online Community

Jennifer K. Tweedy, MS Tech

SOCIAL MEDIA AND THE PUBLIC HEALTH SPHERE

People form and engage around ideas, topics, and needs in online social spaces. They consume news and information, share opinions, find resources, and connect with other individuals and brands. Public health populations are no different. Belonging to communities of individuals with interests and passions in common is a strong draw of social networks. With approximately 75% of the online adult population using social media,[1] the days have passed when organizations can wave off an online social presence, unwilling to dedicate resources to an unknown entity.

Communication via social media affords the public sector a low-cost and potentially broad-reaching opportunity to interact directly with audience segments and build community in customer-chosen online environments in which they are comfortable. Social media flattens a diverse landscape of geographic, social, and economic barriers, enabling the individual with community, reach of voice, and efficient consumption of information from multiple channels. A connected citizen or customer is an empowered one.

DIVERSITY IN SERVICES AND AUDIENCE

As one of the largest and most diverse Arizona state agencies, the Arizona Department of Health Services (ADHS) provides services and regulatory authority for a breadth of public health initiatives and programs serving numerous audiences. Areas of focus include public health prevention and preparedness, licensing of facilities and some healthcare providers, and the state behavioral health system. ADHS entities include the psychiatric Arizona State Hospital and the Arizona State Laboratory.

ADHS regulatory responsibilities extend to the licensing of numerous facilities and groups, including childcare and nursing home centers, midwives, and emergency medical technicians; administration of the Arizona Medical Marijuana Program for patients, caregivers, and dispensaries; and oversight of statewide behavioral health services.

Among the public health preparedness efforts are epidemiology and disease surveillance, and preparation and response to public health emergencies such as the H1N1 virus in 2009. The Department also publishes statistics on a variety of public health measures and trends and administers vital records, including birth and death certificates.

Access to healthcare, especially for vulnerable and uninsured populations; raising awareness of chronic diseases such as heart disease, cancer, and diabetes; smoking prevention and cessation; and promoting physical activity and nutrition education are some of ADHS's public health prevention efforts.

Potential ADHS audience segments include health professionals; licensees for adult, juvenile, and child care facilities; individuals in need of care for family members; recipients of behavioral health services; parents seeking newborn screening requirements and vaccination recommendations; those seeking disease information and wellness services; researchers gathering demographic statistics; and those who qualify for low-income assistance through programs such as Women, Infants and Children (WIC).

Unlike many organizations using social media to market a tightly defined family of products, ADHS offerings and audience are highly diverse. A significant part of the organization's marketing efforts is in the realm of public health awareness and prevention to affect positive behavior changes, which occupies much of the online social strategy. Sharing information about ADHS initiatives and encouraging public feedback is another significant focus.

The presence of ADHS in print, television, radio, outdoor advertising, promotional items, and websites must reflect the diversity of the audience. ADHS uses social media as an extension of other marketing efforts and online resources, which contributes to the expansion of reach beyond that afforded by traditional media. The organization engages with citizens in the online environments of their choosing, allowing for communication of messaging, resources, and services to the fullest extent, and strives for meaningful social exchanges, resulting in real, authentic, relevant conversations with the people of Arizona.

FOCUS IN THE ONLINE SOCIAL SPACE

ADHS is active in blogging, micro-blogging, image and video sharing (including live broadcasting of public events), professional and social networking platforms, and online forums. Many of the usual channels are represented: Twitter®, Facebook, Google+, YouTube, Livestream, Vimeo®, Pinterest, Flickr®, Instagram®, Picasa, UserVoice, and LinkedIn®. The organization uses content in these social media spaces externally with the public community and internally with employees by embedding photo and video content on the ADHS Intranet, where employees comment and engage around a variety of topics.

ADHS contributes public health messaging from many of its programs across social media channels and uses Twitter for real-time conversation about public events and health topics. Twitter chats discussing the importance of vaccines for infants and Valley Fever awareness (Fig. 8-1) are two instances.

Figure 8-1. The ADHS Valley Fever Twitter Chat.

The ADHS YouTube channel (http://youtube.com/azdhs) includes commercials and public service announcements, event recordings, and timely messages from ADHS Director Will Humble (Fig. 8-2). At the time of this writing, video views on the ADHS YouTube channel are more than 4.9 million. The video content is used across the Department's online properties.

Figure 8-2. The ADHS YouTube Channel.

Power Me A2Z and Project Quit are two initiatives for which ADHS has used its Facebook presence (http://facebook.com/azdhs) for campaign-specific communication. The Bureau of Nutrition and Physical Activity popularizes the importance of multivitamins with women of childbearing age through the Power Me A2Z project (Fig. 8-3). Outreach to female college students via in-class materials, online ads targeting young women in Arizona, and traditional media amplify traffic to the Power Me A2Z Facebook tab (http://bddy.me/1693cfy). ADHS encourages participants to share video diaries on several questions, including "What does it mean to you to be healthy?" The campaign is newly launched at the time of this writing and ADHS plans to magnify earned media across ADHS social properties to expand engagement.

Project Quit from the Bureau of Tobacco and Chronic Disease tracks the tobacco cessation journey of four individuals through video blogs. The Facebook tab

Figure 8-3. Power Me A2Z Facebook Tab.

(http://bddy.me/12pCGQA) incorporates video stories of campaign participants, links to expanded tobacco cessation resources, and offers registration to receive information by email. Rotating features include a pledge for tobacco cessation that users share with their friend base and a public poll with real-time results that asks people to give their top reason for wanting to quit tobacco.

The *ADHS Director's Blog* (http://directorsblog.health.azdhs.gov) is an extension of the resources and services offered through other websites and materials. Director Will Humble and his leadership team promote a culture of transparency, which the blog supports. This online property provides the opportunity to share the backstory about current public health events, legislation, the processes surrounding ADHS efforts, and the motivations for public health initiatives. The *Director's Blog* humanizes the efforts of the organization, presenting to the online community a person with whom they can connect. Through a blog post from Director Humble about school nutrition, a Twitter conversation with a Valley Fever expert, or a video of employees volunteering time at a local food bank, ADHS ceases to be a logo or program title and becomes a network of human beings working for the community.

The ADHS Pinterest page (http://pinterest.com/azdhs) features a variety of content related to programs and services, including community involvement efforts, ADHS smartphone apps, and other audience- and topic-based boards such as resources for healthy aging. Parents can obtain immunization schedules, mothers can locate breastfeeding support, seniors can find resources on health screenings and injury prevention, children can play games around healthy eating choices, and teens can hear the voice of Tobacco Addiction and be exposed to a myriad of reasons not to start using tobacco. Pinterest also offers an avenue to increase transparency about strategic community planning to improve population health, as well as campaigns such as increasing awareness and success rates of Hands-Only CPR.

ADHS engages with the community wherever they may be online. Messaging from the organization is no longer a one-way push of information via a brochure in a waiting room of a doctor's office, on a billboard along the highway, in an op-ed in the Sunday newspaper, or in a commercial during the evening news. ADHS connects with people and has conversations on their terms.

The agency considers email marketing to be a strong resource in the communications toolkit. Although not truly social because of its one-way dissemination of information, email allows the reach of a specific segment of an online community and regular delivery of in-depth, topic-specific resources (Fig. 8-4). It is another avenue for communication and outreach, and ADHS maintains multiple campaigns targeting numerous audience segments.

Popular email campaign topics range from news releases from the Public Information Office and healthy recipes from the Bureau of Nutrition and Physical Activity to more niche publications such as Environmental Lab updates and the Arizona Healthcare Connection, which addresses a shortage of healthcare providers for vulnerable populations. Among other topics are summertime heat alerts for school representatives and updates for child-care providers participating

Figure 8-4. Sample email and Pinterest pins popularizing healthy recipes.

in the ADHS Empower Program, which encourages children to make positive choices in nutrition and physical activity and teaches the harmful effects of tobacco use. The Department expands its online community by linking to social media channels from email communications, driving traffic to email subscription options from social media, and reinforcing the content shared between online social and email marketing efforts.

ADHS experiences varying levels of engagement in social networks, and the channels provide overlapping reach to various online audience segments. The approach to adopting platforms is not expansion for the sake of expansion; the goal is to allocate resources based on success in attaining the farthest reach of messaging and meaningful interactions.

MEETING SPECIFIC NEEDS

The Department's motivation for using social media is to build community by listening to concerns and interests of the populations served; expanding opportunities for meaningful connections with the community in the online social environments that they choose; increasing the channels by which citizens can reach ADHS; and expanding share of voice and influence related to the public health topics with which ADHS is charged to make positive change.

Two needs have emerged that could be affected by ADHS's social media presence: 1) increasing awareness about the organization and transparency of its efforts, and 2) sharing public meetings with an audience beyond those who physically attend them. Two initiatives meet these goals and exemplify the value of social media to the organization: the birth of the Arizona Medical Marijuana Program and rulemaking for the Arizona Midwifery Scope of Practice.

ARIZONA MEDICAL MARIJUANA PROGRAM

On November 2, 2010, Arizona voters passed the Arizona Medical Marijuana Act, which charged ADHS with implementing the state's Medical Marijuana Program. Throughout the efforts, ADHS used the *Director's Blog* to share information about the various facets of the program. Earlier that year, before passage of the voter initiative, Director Humble shared anticipated stipulations of the law (Fig. 8-5). These included to "administer the registration, application and approval process for users and dispensers; set some of the approval criteria; provide for and administer a renewal application process; set the fees to run the program; issue cards to patients, caregivers, and dispensary employees; register the dispensing facilities; create and manage [a] web-based verification system for law enforcement; and generate an annual report."[2]

Figure 8-5. ADHS *Director's Blog* regarding medical marijuana voter initiative.

In general, the resources shared in this blog environment support the campaigns and services that are communicated elsewhere online and via traditional media, increasing the transparency and visibility of these efforts. The blog proved to be a popular channel for a behind-the-scenes look at the status of the Medical Marijuana Program initiative and a forum for discussion for interested parties.

Ongoing medical marijuana-related topics on the *Director's Blog* include updates surrounding various legal actions related to the program; the intersection of state and federal laws; actions taken against potentially fraudulent physicians and dispensaries; development plans and timelines for qualified patient applicants, caregivers, and dispensaries, and the rollout of online applications in support of these audiences; identification cards; zoning issues; internal ADHS efforts to implement the voter mandate; announcements for public meetings; and online opportunities for the public to comment on proposed draft rules governing the program.

At the end of December 2013, the blog included 150 medical marijuana posts and 2,471 related interactions with the ADHS online community in the form of comments. Traffic to the *Director's Blog* increased 785% over the 6-month period between the first post about the voter initiative in April of 2010 and its subsequent passage, a testament to the reach and effectiveness of this online property.

The popularity of the medical marijuana voter initiative spotlighted the need to increase access to public meetings beyond individuals able to attend in person. Two public meetings were held during development of the program: 1) the Debilitating Conditions Hearing, during which ADHS leadership listened to comments from medical marijuana patient applicants, the medical community, and others interested in the addition of debilitating conditions qualifying for the use of medical marijuana; and 2) the Dispensary Selection News Conference, when ADHS selected medical marijuana dispensaries to operate throughout Arizona.

To expand the reach of these public events, ADHS broadcast them live, which allowed unlimited video access to the proceedings for remote online users and preserved the meetings for public record. An onsite overflow room with video and voice connection accommodated additional people who wished to attend in person and comment publicly but were not able to secure a spot in the primary meeting room. Following each meeting, ADHS added the video stream to the agency's YouTube channel, where all video content is archived and organized by topic playlist (Fig. 8-6).

An online survey supported the collection of public comment about qualifying debilitating conditions under consideration for the Medical Marijuana Program. This allowed the online community to provide feedback beyond public meetings at any time during implementation of the voter-approved act.

ADHS communicated the locations and topics for the public meetings and shared a host of program-related progress and resources via social (Fig. 8-7) and traditional channels. In a series of videos posted to the ADHS YouTube channel and azdhs.gov (Fig. 8-8), Director Humble discussed what citizens could expect from the Department regarding implementation of the law, publicized opportunities for the public to comment on regulations governing the program, and reviewed the timeline for qualified patient, caregiver, and dispensary agent applications.

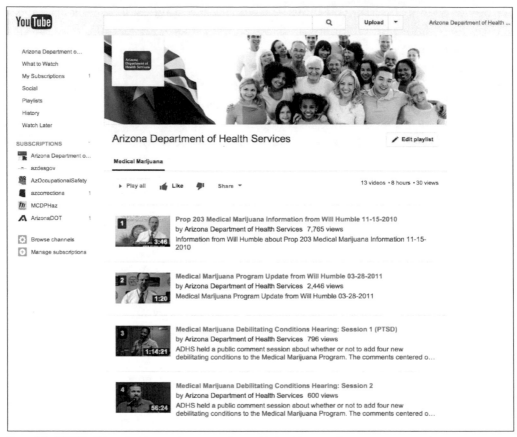

Figure 8-6. ADHS YouTube video library related to the Arizona Medical Marijuana Program.

The ADHS customer feedback forum (http://azdhs.uservoice.com) serves as an outlet for obtaining feedback related to the services offered by the Department. Among the comments may be requests for the status of birth certificates issued through the Office of Vital Records, suggestions for expanding online services, inquiries from students seeking internships, and opinions about resources that ADHS provides. The one-to-many nature of online forums has the advantage of responding in real time to customer feedback and allows ADHS to group related conversations into categories. One of those categories is for the Medical Marijuana Program. A modest knowledge-base of consumer questions and answers grouped from interactions about the program serves as an extension of ADHS online FAQs. At the time of this writing, medical marijuana-related inquiries submitted via this channel are approaching 400. The forum also employs participatory game mechanics in the form of voting. Users can vote on the comments provided by everyone, elevating popular ideas and content to the attention of ADHS and others.

Fig. 8-7. Tweet publicizing the live broadcast of a public hearing.

Figure 8-8. Video of ADHS director explaining the proposed Medical Marijuana Program.

ARIZONA MIDWIFERY SCOPE OF PRACTICE

Arizona Midwifery Scope of Practice Advisory Committee meetings have also garnered high attendance and participation. ADHS regulates licensed non-nurse midwives in the state. In December 2011, midwives and supporters assembled at an ADHS building in Phoenix to protest the regulations that governed their practice at the time (Fig. 8-9). Director Humble asked the group to select a few

Figure 8-9. Protest about the scope of practice for licensed midwives in Arizona.

representatives from those gathered and invited them to his office for a discussion of their concerns.[3]

The result of that initial dialogue and subsequent meetings was Arizona House Bill 2247, introduced in March of 2012, which allowed ADHS to revise the rules governing midwifery practice in Arizona.[4] Over the 6 months following the protest, the Department formed an advisory committee with licensed midwives, a certified nurse midwife, doctors, and members of the public who began meeting regularly to discuss proposed changes to the rules. ADHS began community outreach primarily through social media channels (Fig. 8-10).

Figure 8-10. Tweet advertising an Arizona Midwifery Scope of Practice Advisory Committee meeting.

The audience research and online listening performed at the beginning of the rulemaking initiative revealed modest blogging and Twitter activity among the Arizona midwifery population, and that they were interested in amplifying their efforts using Twitter during upcoming public meetings focused on the rulemaking process. For ADHS, one of the first steps in social communication related to this initiative was to establish a clear and message-neutral hashtag–#azmidwives–which the

Figure 8-11. Post and comments on the *Director's Blog* related to the midwifery rulemaking process.

Department shared in online communications and was quickly adopted by the Arizona midwifery community.

Numerous posts to the *Director's Blog* and extensive comments between the community and ADHS leadership (Fig. 8-11) generated significant interactions. ADHS broadcast six committee meetings live (Fig. 8-12), which included public comment, and tweeted real-time updates during the proceedings.

Figure 8-12. Live broadcast of a Midwifery Rulemaking Committee Meeting.

In an effort to further communication with the public, the agency hosted a live chat on Twitter during one of the first midwifery public meetings to help answer questions in real time and head off any false information being shared. This chat offered yet another forum to share thoughts on the process. It was also an opportunity for ADHS to respond to negative comments with information, facts and resources that substantiated the Department's positions and continued the discussion. Embedding the tweet stream associated with the campaign hashtag next to the live video feed on LiveStream proved advantageous: 79% of non-ADHS-generated tweets during the public meetings containing #azmidwives were published via the ADHS LiveStream channel. Remote viewers watched the broadcast and joined the conversation.

As of June 2013, when ADHS filed the final Arizona Midwifery Scope of Practice, public meetings streamed live and available on-demand on Livestream and YouTube had received more than 6,250 views. This content included a video (Fig. 8-13) of Director Humble published early in the rulemaking process explaining the background of the legislative mandate, describing what could be expected from upcoming public meetings, sharing disparate perspectives from the various audiences with vested interest, publicizing opportunities for public comment (including in-person and online), and offering insight into the Department's rulemaking process.[5]

Figure 8-13. Video of Director Humble explaining the Midwifery Scope of Practice rulemaking process.

Significant input from interested parties was also facilitated by an online survey available during the rulemaking process. Submitted comments and opinion were published to the ADHS website for ongoing review and feedback and helped shape the final rules.

ADHS licenses approximately 60 Arizona non-nurse midwives at any one time, a small group relative to the overall population of individuals and facilities licensed across all agency programs. However, interest in the midwifery rulemaking process reached beyond licensed non-nurse midwives to other audience segments: physicians, registered nurse midwives, and homebirth advocates and supporters. The combination of face-to-face discussions and online social outreach throughout the rulemaking initiative increased awareness, contributed to a wide effort in community building and transparency of process, expanded the reach of messaging, and allowed robust participation by the online community (Fig. 8-14).

Figure 8-14. Sample tweet during the online broadcast of a Midwifery Scope of Practice Advisory Committee meeting.

ADHS CULTURE AND COMMUNITY BUILDING

The success of a brand's online social presence requires that it be a true extension of the philosophy and culture of the organization. ADHS partnership in online social spaces with the various groups invested in the Medical Marijuana Program and Midwifery Scope of Practice is a natural extension of the collaborative involvement outside of social media with the communities served. This reflects deep ADHS commitment to working hand-in-hand with citizens and stakeholders. Social media supports that approach and affords interactions with the Arizona public on their terms.

Part of the commitment to those who interact with ADHS via social media is timely response to both positive and negative feedback. Many of the comments related to medical marijuana and midwifery rulemaking were emotionally charged and not always supportive of state efforts. Rather than shying away from such negative sentiment, ADHS used the opportunity to engage, clarify, and share more information about a topic in question. Responding to feedback offers an opportunity to teach about issues affecting public health, reinforce a particular position with research, or simply acknowledge someone's disappointment in a service provided and make a commitment to do better. Chances are the sentiment shared by an individual is felt by others who chose not to engage directly with the Department. Responding to that person publicly represents communication with all those following a particular topic or thread, builds rapport and trust, and strengthens relationships with the online community. And it can create enthusiastic brand advocates to amplify the message and reach through word of mouth.

The ADHS leadership team operates with an open communication style, welcomes feedback, and promotes high transparency in processes surrounding ADHS efforts, initiatives, and programs. Members throughout the organization understand and embrace the benefits of using social media for online community building. Without this, the success experienced to date may not have been realized.

LOOKING TO THE FUTURE

Although ADHS was an early adopter of social media in Arizona state government,[6] like many organizations, the agency's initial foray into online social media did not involve a robust and formal strategy. Social media use widened the reach of campaigns built on traditional media and websites, but was not immediately integrated into an overarching communication plan. In hindsight, it seems almost impossible to have developed a meaningful approach without first having tried, failed, and succeeded to varying degrees using social media.

Current online social strategy efforts are directed at expanding listening beyond mentions of the brand and internal subject matter experts, public health topic keywords, and trending topics; identifying additional online environments —both expansive and niche — where existing and potential online community members share and consume information; better honing ADHS messaging to specific audience segments in various channels; and capturing warm metrics that measure meaningful interactions with the online community. Identifying brand advocates and key influencers, as well as their passions, agendas and interests to use as potential amplifiers in the ADHS social messaging network is ongoing. And the evolution of the Department's online strategy includes further integration of social media and email marketing. Email can be a powerful reminder to bring people back to a social conversation and a catalyst for sharing content socially.

The tools ADHS uses to measure social media success also have evolved. What satisfied reporting needs in the early days of participation in online social media does not meet the demand for tracking multiple campaigns across channels, websites, and blogs, and capturing warm metrics. ADHS is revisiting and expanding the measure of engagement, sentiment analysis, and share of voice in the public health topics the Department strives to engage in and influence.

COGENT CONNECTIONS

In a congested landscape of social media dos and don'ts, return on "I" acronyms, and the latest increase-your-reach technique, it's easy to lose sight of the most basic of exchanges between brand and customer, and arguably the most important: a conversation. The simplest of exchanges can have a dramatic impact and by the very nature of social media be amplified exponentially by multiple personal networks.

ADHS has had many rewarding exchanges with Arizona citizens through social media. One interaction was with a woman who shared publicly that she was without health insurance and experiencing a difficult time financially. She was a breast cancer survivor, having undergone a mastectomy, was taking medication in support of her recovery, and was in need of follow-up mammography and a visit to an oncologist for renewal of her medication. Responding to an ADHS Facebook post about the Well Woman Healthcheck Program, she asked for information about an affordable option to meet her immediate healthcare needs. ADHS provided her with information about a program close to her home that offered the services she sought as well as additional health screenings potentially appropriate for her and her spouse. Later the same day she reported that she was scheduled with a doctor for the following day.

After all of the strategic work around messaging, campaigns, audience segments, online environments, targeting, technical implementation, and metrics, something basic and über powerful happens that reminds us all why we vaulted into online social media in the first place: we reach out, and someone reaches back with a sincere and important need that we can help with, and we do.

REFERENCES

1. Brenner J, Smith A. 72% of online adults are social networking site users. *Pew Internet*. 2013. http://pewinternet.org/Reports/2013/social-networking-sites.aspx. Accessed November 21, 2013.

2. Humble W. Medical marijuana. *ADHS Director's Blog*, April 22, 2010. http://directorsblog.health.azdhs.gov/?p=243. Accessed November 21, 2013.

3. Humble W. Home birth protest, *ADHS Director's Blog*. December 6, 2011. http://directorsblog.health.azdhs.gov/?p=2047. Accessed November 21, 2013.

4. Arizona Department of State Office of the Secretary of State. *House Bill 2247: An Act Relating to the Licensing and Regulation of Midwifery.* March 26, 2012. http://azsos.gov/public_services/LegislativeFilings/PDFs/2012/50th_Legislature_2nd_Regular_Session/CH_93.pdf. Accessed November 21, 2013.

5. Midwifery Scope of Practice Advisory Committee Meeting – Preview. February 7, 2013, http://www.youtube.com/watch?v=IMFv1nVA9g0. Accessed November 21, 2013.

6. Advice to Consumers: Healthcare 'Friending' Social Media: What Is It, How Is It Used, and What Should I Do?," February 2, 2012, http://www.himss.org/files/HIMSSorg/content/files/HealthcareFriendingSocialMediav15(4).pdf. Accessed November 21, 2013.

Chapter 9:

Why Do I Blog?

David Gelber, MD, FACS

Editors Note: *This chapter shares Dr. Gelber's perspective of using a blog as a professional and at times that also means bringing other interests into the conversation as a way of humanizing him to potential patients. His chapter reflects his strategy and goals for blogging – whether it is connecting with patients, peers, other professionals or all of the above. Keep in mind as you read this chapter that every blog is different – each is a reflection of the blogger and what makes them unique.*

THE BLOGGER

In 2006, I started writing a religious science fiction novel, building on an idea that had been bouncing around in my head for about 30 years. *Future Hope* was published in 2008. The few fans I had, those who had actually read my novel, asked for a sequel, which I dutifully began to write. At the same time, debate began to mushroom about the future of the healthcare industry, a topic close to my heart due, in large part, to my livelihood. I held definite opinions about the current state of healthcare, and after a little research, I wrote my first blog article: *Health Care Debate: The View from the Trenches.*[1] The question remained of where to publish my thoroughly researched and thoughtful article. Without much computer knowledge, I performed some research about blogging and discovered that anyone can set up a blog in a few minutes. I went to Google, followed it to Blogger, and gave birth to *Heard in the OR*. More than 100 articles later I'm still going strong.

WHY BLOG?

Is there a good reason for physicians to have blogs? Why should anyone care what is *Heard in the OR*, the title of my blog (http://heardintheor.blogspot.com/)? Following are my reasons for continuing.

I blog to voice my opinions on topics of the day that are important to me. I've posted thoughts on the healthcare crisis, global warming, wild horses, and so much more, always trying to add a touch of humor and my own special insight. For example, my observations and solution to global warming can only be described as unique:

The economic crisis, coupled with the US Congress' attempts to reform health care along with cap and trade have led to unprecedented CO2 release from members of Congress and the Executive Branch. The excessive CO2 emissions have also coincided with a three hundred percent increase in hot air emanating from this region of the country....

The order states that Democrats will only be allowed to exhale on Mondays, Wednesdays and Fridays. Republicans will have exhalation rights on Tuesdays, Thursdays and Saturdays. Sundays have been deemed a day of rest and no exhalation will be allowed by members of congress from either party on this day. – from *Global Warming*.[2]

I blog to tell a story. I began my second career writing fiction. If nothing else, I've been told I have a creative, although sometimes bizarre imagination. Often I am hit by an idea at the oddest times, possibly while I'm deep within someone's pelvis wrestling with his or her colon or perhaps standing in the shower. Wherever and whenever my "muse" strikes, I do my best to remember the idea and build upon it. I've published stories and parables on my blog from installments of the eschatological *The Lost Light*[3] to *More Things*,[4] a parable about our materialistic world, to *Fifteen Minutes*[5] about an individual's thoughts as he faces his impending death. Sharing these stories brings me some feedback, and I hope I'm providing some entertainment and a bit of education to my few faithful readers.

I blog to educate my readers, primarily about the practices and pitfalls in the world of surgery. I've been a practicing surgeon for more than 20 years. I've seen the mundane and the peculiar, saved lives, stamped out disease, cured cancer, drained gallons of pus, repaired broken bodies, and cared for some of the sickest people imaginable. Most people outside of the healthcare world have little or no idea of the challenges that physicians face every day. One of my tasks is to teach the average person what it means to be a surgeon. *On Surgery*[6] presents the odd combination of arrogance and humility that surgeons must possess. *Under the Drapes*[7] discusses the unique dedication of the surgeon. Woven throughout my medical writing is the sense of wonder I experience at the remarkable way *Homo sapiens* are constructed. The human hand, our eyes, even the little known omentum, which resides within the abdomen, and so much more are examples of that amazing construction. If I can share this knowledge with just one reader, I believe I've accomplished a major goal.

I admit that I blog to advertise. I've found the writing part of authorship and publishing to be relatively easy. Except for finding enough time in the day, I have no trouble committing words to the computer screen. *On Writing*[8] explored the process I go through with each of my literary creations, but making the world aware of the existence of my golden prose has never been my strong suit. Although I may appear verbose in the written word, I am not much of a talker, nor am I outgoing.

With the blog, I can write something funny, entertaining, or pertinent to the modern world and people throughout the world can read and maybe even like it. Perhaps they want to read more of what I've written. Thus, the blog becomes a powerful marketing tool. I currently have about 10 to 20 visitors to my blog daily. Sometimes my articles are picked up by larger social media sites and the blog traffic grows accordingly. As blog traffic increases, awareness of my other writing grows and book sales may increase.

I blog to vent my frustration over the inanities that exist in today's world of medical care. Most people don't realize this, but the healthcare industry is, for the most part, under the control of the federal government. Payments to doctors at least are tied to Medicare, which is a government program. All reimbursement is controlled similarly because almost all insurers tie their reimbursement rate to Medicare. One consequence is that hospitals and doctors are frequently asked to jump through a variety of hoops to qualify for a variety of payment incentives. Tasks such as filling out mountains of superfluous paperwork, following poorly conceived or inappropriate protocols, or providing page upon page of unnecessary documentation to satisfy a government mandate are taking doctors and nurses away from their truly important duty of caring for the sick and injured. Blog articles such as *Inquisition*,[9] *Obamagolf*,[10] and *What About the Patient*[11] recount some of my frustrations with the system in which I am forced to practice today. Those in power have burdened the healthcare system with a mountain of bureaucracy that contributes nothing to the well-being of the patients, while serving to frustrate those on the frontlines of medicine.

I blog to have a bit of fun. Although most people would not consider writing to be fun, sometimes I write things for myself, only sharing the words with the world as an afterthought. My entire short novel *Minotaur Revisited* belongs in this category. I began it as a short satirical piece retelling the Minotaur myth from the *true* perspective of the Minotaur, the half-man/half-bull beast imprisoned within the Labyrinth on the Greek island of Crete. In my version the Greek hero, Theseus, is the true cad, while Quint, the Minotaur, is a truly noble monster. The Minotaur secretly escapes his Labyrinth prison and enters the world. I kept him alive for thousands of years, allowing him to interact with history, meeting historical figures from Moses to Mama Cass.

Another blog post, *After Horton*[12] is my satirical take on Dr. Seuss, recounting the story after the story, in this case the events that occurred after *Horton Hears a Who.* For those of you who never read Dr. Seuss, Horton is an elephant who hears the voice of the Mayor of Whoville, a tiny, tiny village situated on a dust speck. Horton goes to great lengths to save this tiny enclave of humanity that only he, by virtue of his enormous ears, can hear. In my blog article, Horton goes on to star in Tarzan movies and Jo Jo Who, whose timely "Yopp" saved the Whos from disaster in the original book, goes on to rock stardom, only to die tragically of an overdose of heroin. I suppose I have a jaded perspective on our world to speculate on the tragedy that occurs after the parades and celebrations are finished. Unfortunately, it is far too common for spectacular success to lead to even more spectacular failure.

Finally, I blog to offer my observations on the physical and spiritual world that surrounds us. When I sit outside my home and watch the activity in my backyard or jump out of my car to save a turtle trapped in the road or observe the behavior of my numerous dogs and birds, I am usually struck by the marvels of our world. *Backyard Nature*[13] and *Man's "Best" Friend: The Noble Basset Hound*[14] offer my commentary on the world around me. It is filled with hummingbirds, lizards, birds, dogs, and so much more that amazes me. If I can share this wonder and amazement with others, I believe I've accomplished an important task.

I suppose my blogging is rather different from the usual weblog that chronicles a trip or some other adventure. My goal is to share my joy and sense of awe of the world of surgery and the world in which we live while pointing out the many foibles that combine to make the human race.

REFERENCES

1. Gelber D. Health care debate: the view from the trenches. *Heard in the OR*. 2009. http://heardintheor.blogspot.com/search?q=from+the+trenches. Accessed November 22, 2013.

2. Gelber D. Global warming. *Heard in the OR*. 2009. http://heardintheor.blogspot.com/search?q=global+warming. Accessed November 22, 2013.

3. Gelber D. The lost light. *Heard in the OR*. 2011. http://heardintheor.blogspot.com/search?q=last+light. Accessed November 22, 2013.

4. Gelber D. More things. *Heard in the OR*. 2010. http://heardintheor.blogspot.com/search?q=More+things. Accessed November 22, 2013.

5. Gelber D. Fifteen minutes. *Heard in the OR*. 2013. http://heardintheor.blogspot.com/search?q=fifteen+minutes. Accessed November 22, 2013.

6, Gelber D. On surgery. *Heard in the OR*. 2009. http://heardintheor.blogspot.com/2009/12/on-surgery.html. Accessed November 22, 2013.

7. Gelber D. Under the drapes. *Heard in the OR*. 2012. http://heardintheor.blogspot.com/search?q=under+the+drapes. Accessed November 22, 2013.

8. Gelber D. On writing. *Heard in the OR*. 2012. http://heardintheor.blogspot.com/2012/09/on-writing.html. Accessed November 22, 2013.

9. Gelber D. Inquisition. *Heard in the OR*. 2013. http://heardintheor.blogspot.com/search?q=inquisition. Accessed November 22, 2013.

10. Gelber D. Obamagolf. *Heard in the OR*. 2013. http://heardintheor.blogspot.com/search?q=obamagolf. Accessed November 22, 2013.

11. Gelber D. What about the patient? *Heard in the OR*. 2013. http://heardintheor.blogspot.com/search?q=what+about+the+patient. Accessed November 22, 2013.

12. Gelber D. After Horton. *Heard in the OR*. 2010. http://heardintheor.blogspot.com/search?q=after+horton. Accessed November 22, 2013.

13. Gelber D. Backyard nature. *Heard in the OR*. 2010. http://heardintheor.blogspot.com/search?q=backyard+nature. Accessed November 22, 2013.

14. Gelber D. Man's "best" friend: the noble basset hound. *Heard in the OR*. 2010. http://heardintheor.blogspot.com/search?q=the+noble+basset+hound. Accessed November 22, 2013.

Chapter 10:

Social Media Hubs: Strategy and Implementation

John Sharp, MSSA, PMP, FHIMSS

Your healthcare organization has official accounts on Facebook, Twitter®, LinkedIn®, and YouTube. You have created a social media policy. You have one person or a small group responsible for social media. You have addressed the items in Table 10-1.

Table 10-1. Checklist for Developing a Social Media Hub

1.	Create the major social media tools and brand them consistently (Twitter, Facebook, YouTube, LinkedIn)
2.	Select a blogging tool for your hub , eg., Wordpress
3.	Assemble a team – writer/editor for the blog, designer, and content experts
4.	Develop a design that is focused around the blog postings but includes your other social media content. Enable the embedding of video and graphics into the site
5.	Develop an editorial calendar – decide how frequently to post on the blog and social media, content to feature which reflects your organization, and who will write each item
6.	Launch the hub, promote on your social media channels
7.	Keep your content fresh, obtain feedback from your readers, monitor social media and metrics to measure what works and what doesn't

Taking social media to the next level means creating real consumer engagement. How does an organization truly engage healthcare consumers online? What are these people seeking and what can the institution provide to create a dialogue?

Social media provides an online platform to develop a dialogue and promote a two-way channel that is not available through traditional media or static website content. In fact, as many have discovered when monitoring social media, your organization probably already is being discussed within the social media sphere, so it makes good sense to join in and guide the discussion.

The first step is to establish a goal of consistent customer engagement that is responsive and relevant. Keeping the focus on patient and consumer needs while staying in line with the organization's mission can be a challenge and building new content can be costly. However, careful planning and content development can feed the needs of your consumers, resulting in significant brand-building benefits. Social media can allow you to direct consumers to quality content generated by others or to provide commentary on current issues such as research studies and new discoveries.

Content marketing, which is the sharing of media and publications in a variety of formats to communicate with customers and prospects, is a key trend for healthcare social media that merits attention.

WHAT IS A SOCIAL MEDIA HUB?

The solution to combining content marketing and patient engagement is a social media hub. The spokes are the four primary social media tools mentioned previously, with others added as desired. The center is a content development area, preferably a blog written by medical or other content experts. Content contributors can include key physicians, nutritionists, and other healthcare professionals. Such contributors should be not only those interested in blogging but those whose messages fit with the organization's communication strategy. An organization that is promoting community health might have a primary care physician, nutritionist, and exercise physiologist join the team of bloggers. A focus on children needs input from a key pediatrician. If disseminating information about specialty care is the goal, such as cardiology or orthopedics, specialists in those areas should be tapped.

Because many, if not all, of those contributing content may be new to blogging, they need to receive content and writing standards. Such standards provide guidance to those writing posts and help ensure consistent branding. Appropriate topics include

- Length of blog posts
- Suggested reading level, including examples
- Topics and priorities
- Style guidelines for your brand
- Frequency of postings
- How to profile the contributors
- How to include videos and photos on the blog or within posts
- Mobile-enabled specific information

Once you have identified your team and designated a writer/editor to manage the content, consult with your information technology team on the necessary technology. Determine whether the envisioned blog can be deployed within the content management system of your existing website or requires a separate but branded Wordpress (http://wordpress.com/) blog. Enhance your hub with widgets, such as adding a twitter stream or highlighting your other social media channels. Establish how the social media hub and content will drive consumers to your website for additional information and scheduling appointments.

The social media coordinator can develop a publication schedule and begin the work of making the hub a reality. The publication schedule should include not only the blog posts themselves but also posting of the blog link to other social media channels and cross-promotion of other social media postings.

The final step is monitoring. The basic level of monitoring is to read and respond to social media, including comments on Facebook posts, retweets on Twitter, and comments on the blog. Establish a procedure to address complaints quickly and offline. Other monitoring should include web analytics of the blog, the volume of social media traffic, and how social media accounts are growing, such as an increase in the number of followers on Facebook and Twitter or the number of hits to videos on your YouTube channel. Traffic from your social media accounts to your website need to be measured: the number of users who click through to view content on your website in addition to your blog. Some use free online tools such as Klout (http://klout.com/home) to monitor their Klout score compared to others, but information provided by these tools is more helpful when users understand the algorithms being used to measure influence. Another approach is to conduct sentiment analysis on your social media. Some free tools are available, but more sophisticated analysis is available by contracting with groups who specialize in social intelligence. Examples of tools are

- Twitalyzer at: http://twitalyzer.com/ (free)
- Socialmention* ar: http://www.socialmention.com/ (free)
- Lithium at: http://www.lithium.com/ (licensed)
- SAS® Sentiment Analysis at: http://www.sas.com/text-analytics/sentiment-analysis/index.html (licensed)

CLEVELAND CLINIC HEALTHHUB

The primary strategy of the Cleveland Clinic HealthHub (health.clevelandclinic.org) (Fig. 10-1) is content and brand journalism to engage patients,[1] which makes sense for a hospital with sufficient existing content and the ability to build new content. The Cleveland Clinic website has more than 15,000 pages of content and 1,000 videos, but the focus of the HealthHub is blogs written by physicians and others that reflect their own interests. The 40 experts represent a range of specialties from oncology and women's health to heart disease and nutrition. With such a broad team of contributors, the content is substantial but also accessible. The content is delivered in brief blog posts of about 300 to 500 words, videos, slide shows, and even infographs. The content may be seasonal ("Seniors: Stay Safe In the Heat") or address issues in dealing with chronic conditions ("How do I tell my children I have cancer?"). True to the Cleveland Clinic focus on wellness, nutrition and exercise comprise a major share of these blogs, addressing childhood obesity and providing healthy recipes and exercise both for healthy adults and children and those living with chronic diseases. In addition, the blogs discuss issues in the news, such as new discoveries at Cleveland Clinic and from recent medical journals. The blogs may post as frequently as 2 to 5 per day and conclude with links to additional website content, such as "The Healthy Pregnancy Guide" or "Helping Overweight Kids Make Healthy Changes."

Figure 10-1. The HealthHub from Cleveland Clinic. Copyright Cleveland Clinic. Used with permission.

The content strategy employed by the Cleveland Clinic has many advantages. Because hospitals cannot make retail offers, the primary marketing strategy is via information and education. This not only results in a more educated audience but builds the brand based on medical expertise that is at a human level. The physician experts are part of the brand, and the content they provide enhances both their personal and the institutional brands. The blend of a personal approach and medical expertise is the most attractive combination in healthcare today.

As part of the strategy, the Facebook page posts links back to the HealthHub and allows comments from users.

In its first year, HealthHub grew to more than 500,000 visits per month. In addition, the Clinic's Facebook page has grown to 450,000 fans (https://www. facebook.com/ClevelandClinic).[2] Forty percent of the hub traffic is from mobile devices. The growing popularity of the HealthHub drives traffic to the website and online appointments. For example, a recent post on irritable bowel syndrome brought this comment, "My daughter has had issues with her stomach since birth can you help her we live in Cleveland we have been to all kinds of doctors."

SEATTLE CHILDREN'S

Seattle Children's Hospital has two blogs. "On the Pulse" (http://pulse. seattlechildrens.org/) includes a variety of topics written by professional writers but quoting physicians, dietitians, and other health professionals. The posts at the time of this writing were 1 to 3 per week. The site also includes a Twitter feed (https://twitter.com/@PediatricPulse) and blog comments but not a clear integration with Facebook. However, the Facebook site (https://www.facebook. com/SeattleChildrens) points to their Storify site (https://storify.com/) for quick tips. The second blog is Seattle Mama Doc™ (http://seattlemamadoc.seattlechildrens. org/) (Fig. 10-2), authored by the nationally known Dr. Wendy Sue Swanson. This blog has numerous photos, a twitter stream, and comments, but it also lacks videos and integration with Facebook. Posts are once or twice per week.

Figure 10-2. Written by Dr. Wendy Sue Swanson, pediatrician and author of Seattle Mama Doc™, a Seattle Children's Hospital blog.

BOSTON CHILDREN'S HOSPITAL

Thriving is the well-developed blog from Boston Children's Hospital (http://childrenshospitalblog.org/) that includes physicians as guest bloggers, an occasional video, and photos with each posting. The postings are 2 to 3 per week, with one physician blogger who also posts on Boston.com and Huffington Post. The posts take advantages of links back to website content and physician profiles. One post on Down syndrome (Fig. 10-3) generated significant interest and was picked up by national news outlets.[3]

LESSONS LEARNED

The Facebook strategy at the Cleveland Clinic is typical of lessons learned in their entire social media strategy.[4] The primary lesson was not to listen to the experts and the key positive lessons were to focus on your expertise and stay true to your mission. That translates into identifying experts to contribute content, especially to blogs; developing new content, including videos, slide shows, and infographs; and keeping content true to the organization's strategic objectives. The Seattle Mama Doc blog has garnered national attention with frank advice on children's health and created a substantial social media presence. Parents frequently looking online for this type of advice gravitate to trusted sources. Boston Children's also focuses on topics of interest to parents of sick children and has generated news coverage from posts that tell real stories of living with chronic conditions.

Figure 10-3. Thriving blog from Boston Children's Hospital.

Staying true to your mission involves aligning your social media strategy with your corporate and community strategy. Social media can give patients and the community a more intimate look what is going on inside the institution through videos, blog posts, and tweets.

Another important factor is to understand how your customers experience your social media communications. Are they engaging? What's the best way to survey consumer needs? What posts are popular and reaching a broader audience? Cleveland Clinic had a surprising experience with a video promoting empathy among employees (http://www.youtube.com/watch?v=cDDWvj_q-o8&feature=youtu.be). The video went viral on social media and presented an unexpected opportunity to capture some of the viewers on HealthHub.[5] The video passed 1 million views on YouTube and generated more than 350 comments.

Finally, be prepared to innovate, whether that means experimenting with new social media tools such as Pinterest or Storify or developing mobile apps that have a unique appeal.

Social media will continue to grow in importance in healthcare relationships. Health systems can use strategies such as social media hubs to engage their communities.

REFERENCES

1. Working R. Cleveland Clinical launches HealthHub content portal. *Ragan's Health Care Communication News.* 2012. www.healthcarecommunication.com/Main/Articles/8786.aspx. Accessed December 2, 2013.

2. Justice J. The big brand theory: Cleveland Clinic employs news-you-can-use to begin social relationships. *Socialmedia Today*. 2013. http://socialmediatoday.com/joan-justice/1524206/big-brand-theory-cleveland-clinic-employs-news-you-can-use-begin-social-relatio. Accessed December 2, 2013.

3. Dkotko B. Mock my pants, not my sister. *Thriving*. 2011. http://childrenshospitalblog.org/mock-my-pants-not-my-sister/. Accessed December 2, 2013.

4. Linabarger S. *Facebook: Doing it Wrong, Getting it Right*. 2013. http://www.slideshare.net/bdionline/facebook-doing-it-wrong-and-getting-it-right-bdi-41713-content-marketing-summit. Accessed December 2, 2013.

5. Pogorelc D. How a tear-jerking Cleveland Clinic video went viral by accident. *MEDCITY News*. 2013. http://medcitynews.com/2013/09/how-a-tear-jerking-cleveland-clinic-video-went-viral-on-accident/. Accessed December 2, 2013.

Chapter 11:

Using Social Media for Research: Addressing Regulatory Challenges

Timothy M. Hale, PhD; Melissa Abraham, PhD, MS; Shiyi Zan; Kamal Jethwani, MD, MPH

One potential use of social media is to educate and motivate patients to undertake healthy behaviors. This may be a particularly relevant approach for adolescents, for whom social media may be the primary form of communication. To this end, we conducted a research study investigating the use of a Facebook intervention to improve asthma control among teens. Using Facebook for a health intervention program poses specific challenges, including securing Institutional Review Board (IRB) approval for the study. Concerns about privacy, security, and protection of study participants with the use of Facebook and other social media for research purposes must be addressed. Social media holds great potential for research and health intervention programs but requires unique navigation of the IRB approval process.

THE HEALTHCARE PROBLEM

Asthma is the most common chronic condition affecting children in the United States, with more than 10 million people younger than the age of 18 (14%) reporting having received a diagnosis.[1] Compared to adults, children are at a greater risk of having an asthma attack and asthma-related hospital visit, accounting for an estimated $56 billion in healthcare costs annually.[2] In 2009, 1 in 5 children with asthma visited emergency departments because of asthma attacks and nearly 50% missed 1 or more days of school.[3] Furthermore, the prevalence of asthma among children has been shown to be higher in the Northeast (>9.8%) compared with the rest of the United States and is of growing concern as rates continue to increase.[1]

Despite the burden posed by asthma, the disease generally can be well controlled if patients take their prescribed controller medications and closely monitor their condition.[4] Healthy People 2020 objectives highlight the need to improve patient education to recognize early signs and symptoms and have physicians assess asthma control more frequently.[5]

One strategy to improve asthma control is the use of questionnaires to assess changes in symptoms that indicate a risk of an asthma attack. The Asthma Control Test (ACT) is a short symptom-based questionnaire consisting of five items that assess asthma symptoms, the use of rescue medications, and the effect of asthma on daily functioning. The ACT has been demonstrated to be reliable and valid and offers a measurable assessment of changes in asthma control over time.[6-9] Results from the ACT have also been shown to correlate with better treatment decisions by clinicians when compared with conventional clinical tests (i.e., spirometry, peak expiratory flow rate, fractional exhaled nitric oxide), which take more time to administer and are often not readily accessible in a primary care setting.[10] Despite such benefits, the utility of the ACT has been limited by its mode of administration, which has traditionally been by a paper format during scheduled office visits. Improving accessibility of the ACT, administering it more regularly, and using automated scoring to provide instant feedback on current status and trends could aid in gauging the success of therapeutic interventions and identifying early signs of deterioration in asthma control.

Social media is a novel approach for improving teens' adherence to monitoring by making the ACT readily accessible. We know that 95% of teens use the Internet and 81% use some type of social media, with 67% reporting that they use social media at least once a day.[11] Among teens who use social media, 94% report having a Facebook account, making it a prime channel for reaching this target population.[11] Teens are active social media users: 88% report sending instant messages, 87% have commented on a friend's post, 86% have posted a status update, and 80% have posted a photo or video online.[12] Social media is also useful for creating and maintaining social networks that are important in the spread of health behaviors.[13-15] Using Facebook to create social networks of teens who have asthma may reinforce treatment adherence and result in better asthma control.

We proposed a research study that would use social media to intervene and engage teens in the control of their asthma, selecting Facebook because of its high rate of adoption by teens. Our initial intervention strategy was to invite teens to join a Facebook group, loosely moderated by a member of the research staff who posted topics for discussion and encouraged participation, and ask them to use a Facebook app to take the ACT. Connect 2 My ACT (C2MA) was envisioned as a 12-month, two-arm, randomized, controlled trial consisting of 120 teens with asthma recruited from patients through the Massachusetts General Hospital Department of Pulmonology and the Pediatric Asthma group. Study participants would be randomly assigned to the intervention group using Facebook or to a control group receiving usual care. The goal was to use Facebook as a means to communicate with teens, regularly administer the ACT, and send alerts when asthma control was poor. Additionally, we hoped that bringing teens together on Facebook would foster a sense of community and social support to reduce stigma associated with asthma and empower teens in self-managing their condition. The primary aim was to examine if participation in the Facebook group improved the management of asthma symptoms, as measured by trends in ACT scores. The secondary aim was to examine if participation in the Facebook group was associated with ACT adherence rates and decreased number of hospitalizations and emergency department visits.

IRB REVIEW AND APPROVAL

This research study required review and approval by the institution's IRB. Research conducted on human subjects is governed by Title 45 Code of Federal Regulations Part 46 and regulated by the Department of Health and Human Services Office for Human Research Protections. These regulations require all research studies to be reviewed and monitored by an independent ethical review board. The IRB is a group either inside or outside of an institution that has the authority to approve research proposals and serves an important role in protecting the rights and welfare of people who participate in research. These regulations were put into place as part of the National Research Act of 1974 in response to the unethical treatment of human subjects in biomedical research (e.g., the Tuskegee Syphilis Study).

Many IRBs in institutions that conduct health research are familiar with the risks and benefits that arise in biomedical research. Research that involves new and changing technologies, however, can be challenging both for IRBs and investigators. Social media is a relatively new domain of communication technology that has been adopted rapidly, especially among younger cohorts, but has not yet been widely used to conduct clinical research. IRBs frequently struggle with understanding how social media platforms such as Facebook function, how information is stored and transmitted, and how to differentiate between private and public information. In addition, social media platforms are constantly undergoing new developments that have potential impacts on the issues that are of concern to IRBs. Faced with these challenges, we approached the IRB staff early in the research design phase to seek their guidance on the ethical, privacy, and data security concerns that might arise when using social media as we planned for our health intervention research study. This initiated a long-term collaboration with IRB staff to revise the research design to ensure that all concerns were addressed.

Although the concept of a Facebook group and dedicated app appears to be a simple and natural solution to address the aims of the study, the use of social media in a clinical research context with minors was novel, and the IRB raised a number of questions about the proposed research design including:

1. The appropriateness of using a social media platform for the study

2. The appropriateness of how health/medical data were transmitted to parties responsible for care

3. Privacy considerations

4. HIPAA and data security issues

5. The informed consent and assent process

Appropriateness of Facebook as a Health Intervention Platform

Before writing the research protocol, study investigators met with IRB staff to determine what issues needed to be addressed to secure IRB approval. One of the first concerns was whether the proposed use of social media would be appropriate for the population and the research problem under investigation as well as its potential risks and benefits to the study population. The IRB recommended considering the proposed research from a participant's perspective to make a case for why the research is appropriate. Primarily, this pertained to whether study procedures were consistent with how a typical individual (in this case, a teen) would use social media. We needed to clarify that Facebook served two purposes: 1) providing a more effective mode of communication to remind teens to complete the ACT, and 2) creating a social environment for teens to interact and share their experiences about living with asthma. In response to guidance from the IRB, we included in the protocol a section that described the general growth of social media, particularly the widespread Facebook adoption rates among the teenage population. We carefully highlighted that social media use has been integrated into the daily lives of teens to justify that the risks of using social media for this research study are in many ways no greater than those most teens encounter in daily life.

To address concerns of how teens might participate in the proposed Facebook group, we conducted a focus group with teens who had asthma. We found that all participating teens in the focus group regularly used Facebook. Although none had previously used Facebook as a tool for learning about asthma or connecting with other teens who had asthma, they expressed interest in learning from a peer role model with asthma who could teach them how to manage their own symptoms better (Table 11-1). Because asthma is a relatively non-sensitive medical diagnosis (as compared to sexually transmitted disease or social anxiety disorder, for example), the sensitivity of sharing personal health information (PHI) was of less concern than it might be with other medical conditions. Therefore, we could argue that creating a Facebook group would contribute to better health outcomes by 1) establishing the equivalent of a "support group" among teens; and 2) providing reminders and easy access to the ACT using a social media platform that teens would find engaging and felt comfortable using in their daily lives. This information provided the IRB with a framework to consider how the "risks" of using Facebook (to privacy) could be outweighed by the health and other benefits of being in the research study. This context is important to describe and convey to the IRB for their deliberations and risk-benefit determinations.

Table 11-1. Excerpted Findings from a Focus Group*

Use of Facebook	"It's the way to communicate." -16-year-old girl "A lot of my classes at school, we have groups on Facebook and we talk about the homework and stuff. So it's easier than texting every single person. And also a lot of people use it if they have a party and want to invite people." -15-year-old girl
Living With Asthma	"I hate feeling sick. I hate feeling out of breath. I don't want to feel that. I just want to feel healthy. I don't want to act sick so I act like I'm fine." -17-year-old boy "Football is supposed to be that big, tough sport. You don't walk into the locker room and say, 'I have asthma.'" -15-year-old boy
Asthma Knowledge	"I really don't know that much about asthma. I just know I've had it since I was young." -17-year-old boy "I'd like to know how to nip it in the bud before it gets too bad. I hate missing school because then I miss cheerleading practice and work and stuff." -16-year-old girl
Perceived Benefits of an Online Asthma Group	"I could learn about when I should use my inhaler. My doctor said, 'Use it when you need it,' but I need him to tell me, 'This is how you'll feel when it's time to use it.'" -16-year-old girl
*Six teens aged 15 to 17 years residing in the Boston area.	

Appropriate Transmission of Health/Medical Data to Parties Responsible for Care

The full value of regular ACT testing would only be realized if clinicians and caregivers had the opportunity to intervene at the correct time. For this reason, we needed to build a service that alerted the teens' care team of critical scores. However, from a technical and legal perspective, the IRB wanted us to consider all the risks and potential harm of such alerts to patients and providers.

In terms of technical architecture, we considered who in the care team should receive alerts and how the alerts should be sent (e.g., phone, email, clinical message). Also, we considered the option of making the alert directly available in the electronic medical record (EMR). We chose the patients' pulmonologist as the gatekeeper for this information and created an alert that would be sent automatically via email. Although clinical messaging would have been ideal for this use, adoption of clinical messaging among clinicians was still low at our hospitals at the time of development, making email a more timely method of communicating with clinicians. We also decided against EMR integration because this would simply make the information available in the record and not help in generating a timely, actionable alert for clinicians. We also wondered whether parents should receive these alerts about their children. To ensure that we were not overwhelming parents with this information, we decided to offer parents a chance to opt out of receiving alerts during the consent process.

From a legal perspective, we needed to ensure that everyone involved was aware of their legal responsibilities during the study. For example, clinicians would be required to address medical issues as they arose and study staff were responsible for reporting all events considered "reportable" to the appropriate bodies, such as potential abuse or unanticipated events. We also included language used during the consent process to make sure that patients were aware that the study was not considered a medical intervention and to reinforce that teens should contact their doctor if their ACT score indicated their asthma was poorly controlled. The IRB also stressed in their review of our study that they would thoroughly evaluate whether the communication of medical data to teens, parents, and clinicians was appropriate.

Privacy Considerations

Issues related to privacy and data security settings received ancillary review by the research computing division of information technology at our institution. This group inquired about Facebook settings, the monitoring and management of the Facebook group, data storage, website and servers, and encryption methods used during data transfer. One of the primary concerns was privacy and the need to understand how Facebook privacy settings function. Specifically, the IRB raised questions regarding whether information about teens' medical conditions, participation in the study group, or interactions with other study participants would be visible to the teens' Facebook connections ("friends") who were not part of the study.

To address this concern, we proposed the use of a relatively little known feature on Facebook: the creation of a private ("secret") Facebook group. To participate in the secret C2MA Facebook group, a teen would be required to be "invited" to the group by study investigators. This approach would restrict participation in the group to only those teens who were part of the research study. In addition, all posts, comments, or "Likes" made within the C2MA Facebook group page would only be visible to other study participants within the group.

However, during the process of creating our study group, we found that Facebook guidelines did not provide sufficient details about how secret groups worked or what data from participation in a secret group was visible to the broader range of Facebook friends. Therefore, our study team devoted considerable time and energy to thoroughly testing the functionalities of a secret group through the creation of a temporary "test" secret group for use among the study team. We simulated a range of common, everyday activities people carry out on Facebook (e.g., posting updates to the group, "Liking" a comment, responding to other comments) and reviewed whether actions and information from the secret group were visible to the wider group of friends. We also tested whether searching in Facebook would reveal the presence of the secret group. This extra precaution was necessary to understand how this feature worked and to ensure that data were not shared outside of the study group. Testing also enabled us to explain these details in the study protocol submitted to the IRB and in the consent form and privacy briefing provided to study participants.

HIPAA and Data Security Issues

A fourth issue that IRB staff raised was how the ACT data would be collected and stored and how we would provide ACT results to teens. Our initial plan was to create a Facebook app that would only be accessible to members of the group. We envisioned this app as a tool to remind teens each month to complete the ACT, administer the ACT, and display to teens the resulting feedback on their current and previous scores. Unfortunately, this approach was quickly determined as unfeasible because Facebook is not HIPAA-compliant, and, thus, PHI could not be collected on Facebook or stored on Facebook servers. In addition, we could not reasonably expect Facebook to change their system to be HIPAA-compliant or enter into a Business Associate Agreement (BAA) as mandated by HIPAA to ensure that PHI is protected when shared between a HIPAA-covered entity (i.e., Partners' research investigators) and business associates (i.e., Facebook).

To circumvent this problem, we created a separate, secure study website to host the ACT questionnaire, store the clinical data, and generate automated alerts for teens and clinicians if ACT scores fell into the critical range. Teens were emailed a unique secure link for access to the site and asked to create a personal password for login. Monthly reminders to take the ACT were posted on the C2MA secret Facebook group page. These reminders also appeared in teens' Facebook "News Feed" pages but were not visible to their wider circle of Facebook friends. Reminder messages with a unique secure link to the study website were also sent to the secret group or to the teens' private Facebook messaging "Inbox." This effectively restricted clinical data access to teens and the study staff, removing Facebook from the process of collecting and storing PHI. Upon clicking the link, teens would be taken to the secure website and asked for their password as authentication.

The IRB also was concerned about the contractors hired to develop the site and where the data would be stored. We ensured that contractors were well-versed in regulations and that the web hosting service had security features and procedures in place that were HIPAA-compliant. Also, all contractors signed a BAA that ensured that they would be subject to the same regulatory considerations as Partners HealthCare.

Informed Consent and Assent Process

The goal of the consent/assent process is to provide people with sufficient information to make an informed decision about participation in a research study. This process involves not only access to details about the study but the opportunity to ask questions to understand fully the purpose of the study, research procedures, and the potential risks and benefits of participating. Because our study required regular access to the Internet to use Facebook, we believed that an online consent/assent process would be appropriate as well as time- and cost-efficient compared to conventional face-to-face consent procedures.

Online informed consent was determined to be appropriate because: 1) there is no other face-to-face interaction involved and having a study visit would create unnecessary burden for the participant, and 2) the study meets minimal risk criteria. Our study met both of these conditions, and the IRB granted a waiver of documentation of informed consent (45 CFR46.117), which allowed us to house our consent document online. We decided to integrate the online informed consent process into the secure study website created to administer the ACT. The recruitment and enrollment workflow was designed so that 1) parents of potential study participants would be contacted by phone to determine interest and eligibility, 2) parents would be sent an email containing a link to the consent form, and 3) once parents consented, teens would be automatically sent an email asking them to create an account and provide their assent to participate. Although the IRB had approved previous projects with an online consent process, they expressed concerns about the process for our study due to the complexity of the study concepts. To meet the IRB's concerns, we divided the consent form into three sections, or web pages, and parents were asked to answer a question at the bottom of each page to demonstrate they had read and understood the information. If they answered incorrectly, they were provided with multiple opportunities to re-read the section and answer correctly before being permitted to move on to subsequent sections. This consent process demonstrated that parents had read the information provided and understood details of the study.

In addition to the informed consent/assent process, we also needed to consider the content of materials provided to potential study participants. These materials were required to provide sufficient information to enable informed, reasoned, and voluntary decisions about participation in the research study. Our institution's IRB provided guidance on online informed consent (Table 11-2) and requested screenshots of the consent form as it would be seen by participants during the study. In addition to details about Facebook privacy in the consent form, the IRB asked that we provide participants with additional information on privacy and security after they had provided their assent to participate. The privacy "briefing" covered in greater detail the steps taken to protect teens' privacy on Facebook, suggestions on how participants could further protect the security and safety of their data, and contact information for additional questions. Participants were required to confirm that they had read and understood this material before being invited to join the Facebook group. The information outlined in the privacy briefing was also used by the IRB to gain a more comprehensive understanding of the proposed method to collect, use, store, and share information in the study.

Table 11-2. Information Required or Requested by IRB When Using Online Consent and Text Examples from the Connect 2 My ACT Study

Information	Text Example
Purpose of the study?	The researchers want to see if regular use of the Asthma Control Test (ACT) by means of Facebook can help teenagers with asthma improve their asthma control.
Why are you asking them to participate?	You are being asked to participate in this study because you have asthma and take daily medication to control your asthma.
How many people will participate?	A total of 120 participants will be enrolled in the study and randomly assigned to one of two groups.
Discussion of extent of confidentiality and data security and risk of breach of confidentiality.	All sensitive information (ACT survey, personal information, etc.) will be stored on a secure database through the study website and available only to study staff to protect the participants' privacy. The risk of this information becoming public is extremely small. If this does occur, we will notify you. However, we cannot predict how information supplied to and stored within Facebook may be used in the future. Currently, all activities on a secret group on Facebook are completely private and protected. Secret groups do not show up on Facebook or internet searches, and the contents of their group pages are only accessible to other group members. In an event that your child "likes" or comments on newsfeeds or group messages, it will remain within the group rather than showing up on a friend's newsfeed. We will update you if these policies change in the future.
Discussion of sensitive information being collected and how this will be handled.	All sensitive information (ACT survey, personal information, etc.) will be stored on a secure database through the study website and available only to the study staff to protect the participants' privacy.
Information about them that will be gathered from other sources.	We will also use the Massachusetts General Hospital AE (Adverse Event) Notification System to track any emergency department visits and hospital admissions to Partners facilities during your child's time in the study. This electronic system lets study doctors know if your child is admitted to a Partners hospital or if your child visits a Partners hospital emergency department for any reason. This alert will let the study doctors know why your child was there. We want to make sure the study doctors know about any possible problems or adverse effects your child may experience while taking part in the study.
Statement that participation is voluntary and they can stop at any time.	Taking part in this research study is up to you and your child. You and your child can decide not to take part. If you and your child decide to take part now, your child can change his/her mind and drop out later by calling the research staff.
Statement that deciding not to participate will not affect the medical care they receive at Partners now or in the future or any benefits they receive now or have a right to receive.	You and your child's decision won't change the medical care he/she gets within Partners now or in the future. There will be no penalty, and your child won't lose any benefits he/she receives now or have a right to receive.
IRB contact information.	If you'd like to speak to someone not involved in this research about your rights as a research subject or address any concerns or complaints you may have about the research, contact the Partners Human Research Committee at 555-555-5555.
Statement informing subjects this is not a medical intervention.	The study itself is not a medical intervention and presents no risks to the participant. Your child will continue to receive usual, standard care from your doctor. If your child's ACT score is below 14, this means that his/her asthma is poorly controlled. If this happens, your child will receive a notification on the study website advising him/her of this condition. Your child will be told to contact his/her doctor. We will send an email to your child's doctor letting him or her know your child's ACT score. We will allow your child's doctor to view all of your child's monthly ACT scores.

PROGRESS REPORT

The study began in December of 2012, and as of September 2013, 70 participants have been enrolled into the study. The current distribution of participants in both intervention and control groups is approximately equal, as is the distribution of participants between the two groups by gender. We hope to complete enrollment by November 2013 and expect the first participants to complete the study in December 2013. Enrollment has progressed smoothly, although getting teenagers to respond to emails and finish each step in the assent and enrollment process has been slightly more difficult than initially anticipated. No intervention participants enrolled on Facebook have reported any technical issues.

In general, teens assigned to the Facebook intervention appear to be taking the ACT regularly and are engaging with the C2MA Facebook group. Although teens do not frequently start new discussion topics, they are willing to engage and make comments once a topic has been initiated. One strategy we have used to engage teens and reinforce key messages has been to post information about celebrities who have asthma (Fig. 11-1). One of our co-investigators, Meghan Searl (using an

Figure 11-1. A post from the study staff (Meghan Harris) on the Connect 2 My ACT Facebook page and reactions of study participants.

account under her maiden name, Harris), moderates the discussions on the C2MA Facebook page and periodically posts to the page to encourage participation. For example, a post about the singer Pink highlights that she has not let asthma keep her from being active in athletics or achieving her goals as a singer. Participants appeared to be surprised to find that some of their favorite celebrities have asthma and were reassured and encouraged to manage their own asthma and achieve personal goals. These types of posts were generally very successful in soliciting comments and "Likes" by study participants.

LESSONS LEARNED

Approximately 12 months elapsed from funding the initial research proposal to receiving final IRB approval to begin recruiting patients. During this time, about 4 months were devoted to early consulting with the IRB staff and revising the intervention strategy and study design. Even with this preparation, IRB approval and subsequent responses to two rounds of questions from reviewers required another 4 months. During this process, we learned many valuable lessons about using social media for health interventions and how best to work with the IRB staff to resolve concerns while maintaining key elements of the research design needed for rigorous testing of our hypotheses. These many lessons can be summarized as seven recommendations:

1. Contact the IRB staff at your institution early in the design phase of research for guidance.

2. Review any institutional or other applicable policies on data security before submitting the proposal, obtaining consultation as appropriate.

3. Review the privacy settings for the social media platform you propose to use and outline what you are doing and why for the IRB.

4. Obtain consultation on HIPAA-related issues; in many cases, a technical issue may be identified that the IRB will want to understand fully.

5. Ask if the IRB has approved similar projects using social media and request copies of approved protocols or other guidance or policies to guide project design.

6. Provide the IRB with a clear, simple description of why the use of social media is integral to and necessary for the research study compared to alternative methods, what potential benefits the use of social media introduces, and how you will mitigate any associated risks.

7. Establish and maintain a good working relationship with the IRB staff. Provide the IRB with a detailed social media plan that includes information on potential issues about which the IRB may inquire. This plan should include who is in charge of the social media platform, how and when it is monitored, how problematic posts are handled, what settings will be used, how data (both PHI and non-PHI) is stored, what happens when you quit or end the study to the information, and explanations in clear terms about who will see what data and when.

CONCLUSION

The popularity of social media channels and services such as Facebook has increased rapidly over the past decade and is all but ubiquitous among some groups. Nearly all teens, for example, regularly and extensively use social media, which has become the primary means by which they connect and communicate with their peers. Although most institutions and corporations have recognized the importance of social media, the healthcare industry has been slow to adopt this communication channel. The need for research on the design and implementation of programs that make effective use of social media to improve healthcare and health outcomes is urgent.

Creating effective health programs requires continuing education for investigators and mutual learning between investigators and IRB staff. Until the use of social media for health intervention research is widespread, investigators need to consider educating the IRB about their research and the issues involved in using social media. Many institutions may have little or no understanding of how social media channels and services work. The rapid and continuing evolution of social media also creates a challenge in keeping up with new services and how they function. Nonetheless, social media is not a fad; it will be a central means of connecting to and communicating with patients for the foreseeable future.

By working closely with our institution's IRB staff, we secured approval to conduct the C2MA study, a health intervention using Facebook for improving teens' adherence to asthma control monitoring. Keys to the success of this process were contacting the IRB early in the study design process, working in a spirit of collaboration and mutual learning, and being flexible in revising study procedures to ensure compliance with federal regulations and ethical guidelines. The future success of research using social media in healthcare requires continued close collaboration between investigators and dedicated IRB staff.

REFERENCES

1. Bloom B, Cohen RA, Freeman G. Summary health statistics for U.S. children: National Health Interview Survey, 2010. *Vital Health Stat 10.* 2011;250:1-80.

2. Moorman JE, Akinbami LJ, Bailey CM, et al. National surveillance of asthma: United States, 2001-2010. *Vital Health Stat 2.* 2012;35:1-67.

3. Centers for Disease Control and Prevention. *Asthma's Impact on the Nation: Data From the CDC National Asthma Control Program.* 2012. http://www.cdc.gov/asthma/impacts_nation/asthmafactsheet.pdf. Accessed June 30, 2013.

4. National Heart, Lung, & Blood Institute, National Asthma Education and Prevention Program. (NAEPP), *Expert Panel Report 3: Guidelines for the Diagnosis and Management of Asthma: Full Report.* Bethesda, MD: US Department of Health and Human Services, National Institutes of Health, National Heart, Lung, and Blood Institute; 2007. http://www.nhlbi.nih.gov/guidelines/asthma/asthgdln.pdf. Accessed December 2, 2013.

5. U.S. Department of Health and Human Services (HHS). *Healthy People 2020 Topics and Objectives: Respiratory Diseases;* 2013. http://www.healthypeople.gov/2020/topicsobjectives2020/objectiveslist.aspx?topicId=36. Accessed July 16, 2013.

6. Juniper EF, O'Byrne PM, Guyatt GH, Ferrie PJ, King DR. Development and validation of a survey to measure asthma control. *Eur Respir J.* 1999;14(4):902-907.

7. Juniper EF, O'Byrne PM, Guyatt GH, Ferrie PJ, King DR, Roberts JN. Measuring asthma control. Clinic questionnaire or daily diary? *Am J Respir Crit Care Med.* 2000;162(4 pt1):1330-1334.

8. Nathan RA, Sorkness CA, Kosinski M, et al. Development of the Asthma Control Test: a survey for assessing asthma control. *J Allergy Clin Immunol.* 2004;113(1):59-65.

9. Schatz M, Sorkness CA, Li JT, et al. Asthma Control Test: reliability, validity, and responsiveness in patients not previously followed by asthma specialists. *J Allergy Clin Immunol.* 2006;117(3):549-556.

10. Ko FWS, Leung T-F, Hui DSC, et al. Asthma Control Test correlates well with the treatment decisions made by asthma specialists. *Respirology.* 2009;14(4):559-566.

11. Madden M, Lenhart A, Cortesi S, et al. *Teens Social Media and Privacy.* Pew Internet & American Life Project; 2013. http://pewinternet.org/Reports/2013/Teens-Social-Media-And-Privacy.aspx. Accessed July 1, 2013.

12. Lenhart A, Madden M, Smith A, Purcell K, Zickuhr K, Rainie L. *Teens, Kindness and Cruelty on Social Network Sites.* Pew Research Center. 2011. http://pewinternet.org/Reports/2011/Teens-and-social-media.aspx. Accessed July 1, 2013.

13. Smith KP, Christakis NA. Social networks and health. *Annu Rev Sociol.* 2008;34(1):405-429.

14. Christakis NA, Fowler JH. The spread of obesity in a large social network over 32 years. *N Engl J Med.* 2007;357(4):370-379.

15. Christakis NA, Fowler JH. The collective dynamics of smoking in a large social network. *N Engl J Med.* 2008;358(21):2249-2258.

Chapter 12:

Legal Aspects of Healthcare Social Media: Staying Out of Trouble

David Harlow, JD, MPH

When the legendary bank robber Willie Sutton was asked why he robbed banks, he gave the straightforward response: "That's where the money is." A similar motivation may be ascribed to healthcare providers who were early adopters of various social media tools. Why be active in social networks? That's where the people are: patients, caregivers, potential collaborators, and referral sources. Facebook has become nearly ubiquitous, and its user base is growing not only among younger people, but also among the older set, who are signing up so they can see pictures of their grandkids. In today's wired society, online social networking is the new word of mouth. Word-of-mouth referrals and personal recommendations have always been prized; many of those conversations simply have moved online.

More than 50% of Americans rely on the internet when looking for healthcare information, and many online searches are conducted on behalf of another person.[1] Most people expect their healthcare providers to be online, providing trustworthy information; the day of the static website has passed. In addition, a growing subset of the population is comprised of "e-patients"[2] who are educated, engaged, and empowered and who seek out healthcare providers prepared to engage with them both in person and online.

Only about 25% of United States hospitals have a social media presence,[3] and a similar proportion of other healthcare providers is likely. Thus, although some providers have been using social media for years, opportunities to reap the benefits of being an early adopter still exist. Even if a provider is not online, others are likely discussing that provider on review sites, Facebook, or even Twitter. Accordingly, providers must at least establish a listening post to keep abreast of what is being posted online. Such monitoring can reveal complaints, recommendations, and other information, allowing the provider to take steps in the real world to ameliorate situations giving rise to complaints and to capitalize on praise and referrals.

Finally, healthcare reform[4] is pushing providers into social media. The Meaningful Use[5] regulations will soon require that providers seeking incentive payments for adoption of electronic medical records make greater use of personal health record portals. In addition programs such as the Medicare Shared Savings Program and Accountable Care Organization[6] program require patient-centeredness and patient engagement,[7] which necessitates the use of online social tools.

With all of these motivating factors, why are healthcare providers slow to endorse social media tools? Numerous legal and regulatory issues are triggered by the use of social media, and some healthcare providers are concerned about the perceived risk. However, remaining uninvolved also has legal and regulatory risks (and attendant market and business risks).

The key issues for consideration include:

- Privacy and security rules under HIPAA[8] as well as other federal and state laws and the ever-diminishing ability to fully de-identify protected health information
- Professional responsibility codes, including both professional society codes of ethics and state regulations promulgated by boards of registration in medicine
- Malpractice liability for professional advice rendered via social media
- Issues raised by daily deal sites such as Groupon®[9] and Living Social, including anti-kickback, fee-splitting, insurance contracts, state insurance laws, and gift certificate laws
- Liability under Federal Trade Commission[10] rules for failure to disclose a financial relationship in conjunction with an online rating, review, or other commentary
- Difficulties with the National Labor Relations Board[11] if employee discussion of working conditions is unreasonably limited (even in non-union shops)

If not managed appropriately, these issues may lead to significant liabilities, ranging from civil and administrative fines to negative publicity and private lawsuits predicated on HIPAA or state law violations. (Even though HIPAA does not provide for third-party liability, some state laws do, and creative lawsuits may seek to add private liability to a HIPAA violation.)

Providers can manage all of these issues by developing comprehensive social media policies that are both outward-facing (i.e., to patients and the general public) and inward-facing (i.e., to physicians, other clinicians, and other staff) as well as tailored to a specific medical practice or other healthcare organization. The policies must be tailored to local conditions because each practice and each healthcare organization is at a slightly different point on its own social media journey. Depending on its comfort level with social media tools and ideas about how to use these tools, each healthcare organization has a unique approach to social media. These differences are natural and should be respected. Due to the legal and regulatory issues involved, it is important for each healthcare organization to involve legal counsel experienced in social media matters in the development and adoption of its policies.

HIPAA AND OTHER PRIVACY CONCERNS

Privacy concerns arising from HIPAA and state privacy laws start from the proposition that only a patient has the right to authorize the release of his or her own private health information. Thus, while an individual patient is free to blog about his or her medical condition or experience with the healthcare system without implicating HIPAA or other privacy rules, provider-generated social media content with identifiable patient information used without consent raises red flags. Provider discussions of cases on social media should follow the "elevator rule" or the "coffee shop rule": If you wouldn't say it in a crowded elevator or coffee shop, don't post it online. As one emergency department physician learned the hard way (she was dismissed by her employer and sanctioned by her state medical board), even a de-identified Facebook post about a patient[12] may easily be re-identified using information from third-party sources. The HIPAA rules[13] list 18 categories of identifying information that must be stripped from a record or patient story for it to be considered de-identified. The 18th category essentially is "anything else that may be used to re-identify the de-identified information." Because the amount of information posted online is regularly doubling, that which is de-identified today may well be easily re-identified tomorrow.

Thus, the best practice is to write about composite/fictionalized patients or obtain patient consent. Providers may wish to rewrite their HIPAA notices of privacy practices to include some level of consent for communication with or about a patient on a particular social media network if that might happen on a regular basis, or if such communication would make sense based on the online activities of the patients and the healthcare organization. For example, an endocrinologist treating teenage patients newly diagnosed with diabetes may consider using Facebook to communicate with patients about managing their diabetes.

Other disclosures made inadvertently also may lead to difficulties. For example:

- A cell phone photo taken in a hospital emergency department of a friend proudly displaying a newly stitched wound may inadvertently capture the image of another patient in the background. That post may be a HIPAA violation attributable to the hospital, even if the organization did not post the photo.

- An employee of a public hospital tweets her displeasure in seeing a clinic staffed up for the convenience of a political figure seeking service off-hours. Her public sharing of identifiable health information led to her being fired.[14]

- Encouraging test results posted by a patient on Facebook might invite response on a human level, but the response must be measured. For example, if a patient posts on a hospital Facebook wall after getting some good test results, "I'm cancer-free 1 year later," hospital staff cannot post much more than "Congrats! Everyone should learn more about early detection on our cancer center's web page." Even if a patient self-identifies first, there is no consent to unlimited public discussion of his or her condition.

PROFESSIONAL RESPONSIBILITY AND MALPRACTICE LIABILITY

Numerous organizations have promulgated social media policies (Table 12-1). Two examples include the American Medical Association (AMA)[15] and the Veterans Administration (VA),[16] which have taken very different approaches. The AMA essentially advocates proceeding with caution and being cognizant of the damage that one's own social media activities and that of one's colleagues may do to the profession. The VA, on the other hand, is out in front on this issue, as it was with electronic medical records, encouraging the use of social media tools to disseminate information and engage patients and caregivers in productive dialogue likely to improve overall well-being and healthcare outcomes.

Table 12-1. Professional Organizations with Social Media Policies and Tools

- American Medical Association
- American College of Obstetrics and Gynecology (*Social Media and Professionalism in the Medical Community* video, also available on YouTube)
- American Nursing Association (toolkit)
- Federation of State Medical Boards
- National Council of State Boards of Nursing
- Veterans Administration

Patient care should not be provided in open social media forums, but appropriate disclaimers on blogs, Facebook pages, YouTube channel pages, and other social media should be sufficient protection for providers seeking to use these tools to share general advice and information.

As in other settings, there are emergency exceptions. If a public social media channel is the only avenue for communicating lifesaving information to a patient, the clinician should not refrain from doing so based on concerns about a privacy violation.

DAILY DEAL WEBSITES

Groupon® (http://www.groupon.com/), LivingSocial® (https://www.livingsocial.com/), and other daily deal websites are being used by healthcare providers, although thus far mostly by those that are not covered by traditional commercial or governmental health insurance (e.g., dental, chiropractic, acupuncture services). This may change as the health insurance landscape changes over time. Resolution of a number of legal issues related to these sites depends, in part, on geographic location because many of the relevant rules are state laws. The questions that arise include:

- Is the 50% of the offer price that Groupon collects as its fee considered illegal fee-splitting under applicable state law?
- Is the 50% fee an illegal kickback in exchange for a referral? Are healthcare providers subject to federal laws in this area in addition to any state laws?

- Do provider agreements with third-party payers prohibit the offering of discounts to plan subscribers? (Providers may need to screen out patients who are insured by carriers that limit their ability to discount or risk being in default under an agreement with their biggest customer.)
- Some states have instituted requirements about expiration dates on gift certificates, and lawsuits have been filed alleging that the relatively short life of the daily deal violates state gift certificate laws.

With the proliferation of high-deductible health plans, flexible spending accounts, and health savings accounts, the general public is becoming more sensitive to prices for healthcare services. Providers are exercising greater creativity to address this issue, but they are subject to a wide-ranging set of regulations above and beyond other consumer-facing businesses.

SOCIAL MEDIA POLICIES AND PROCEDURES

Despite the legal landscape, healthcare providers can develop robust social media programs. The critical first step is to create policies that respect the legal and regulatory limits and are consistent with the organization's level of readiness to engage through social media. Establishing clear guidelines allows clinicians and staff to participate in the online conversation without having to review individual posts with legal and regulatory advisors. An existing policy from another organization may be used as a starting point in the development process, but local customization is key.

An external-facing social media policy should set limits and expectations for people who come to the organization's web properties: web site, Facebook page, blog, YouTube channel, Twitter stream, Google Plus page, Pinterest board, and so on. For example, the policy should note that one who makes a post that violates the terms of service may expect that a hospital whose staff monitors social media accounts at least daily may take down the post (on a forum such as Facebook) if it does not comply with the policy.

An internal set of policies and procedures is also needed to address internal operational and policy issues for both official and unofficial channels to supplement existing personnel policies. At some point in the future, social media issues will not necessarily be called out in a separate category of policies and procedures. However, the range of understanding and comfort with the new and rapidly evolving tools currently varies widely within the workforce and requires specific guidelines. In addition, opportunities to violate the bounds of common sense and employer policies often present in seemingly innocuous ways through the use of social media. For example, LinkedIn® prompts to endorse an individual may lead a user to unwittingly run afoul of an employer's ban on the writing of recommendations by anyone outside the human resources department; accepting a Facebook "friend" request from a patient may be contrary to a clinician's employer's policies; and without proper opt-in procedures, public online conversations may violate applicable laws. Therefore, organizations must address social media issues explicitly with purpose-built policies and procedures.

Staff must be sensitive to the fact that they are, in effect, brand ambassadors on a 24/7 basis. Accordingly, if they mention their employer in posts on their personal Twitter accounts or Facebook pages, such mentions must be consistent with company policy, perhaps noting that "tweets are my own" or words to that effect. Some organizations may want to insist that no employees may discuss the organization except for designated spokespersons. However, National Labor Relations Board (NLRB) rules require that employers may not restrict online discussions of conditions of employment in nonunion as well as union shops. Numerous cases have been decided by the NLRB explicating this rule, and they need to be considered when developing policies and procedures.[17,18]

The best policies are developed through an inclusive process, rather than a top-down process. Employees most likely to be active on social media should be invited to offer input to the process and feel ownership of the final product so as to promote adherence.

No matter what the tenor of an individual organization's policies may be, they must be implemented to be effective. Staff must be trained on the policies and retrained as policies are updated. Because this is a rapidly changing area and comfort levels with social media in an organization may change relatively quickly, these policies should be reviewed at least annually. Adherence to the social media policies should be a condition of employment, just as adherence is required to any other employer policy. Distribution of policy documents and training may be integrated with a broader employment process within the organization.

CONCLUSION

It is too late for any healthcare provider to avoid social media entirely. Even if a practice or institution does not have an active social media presence, most likely others are already discussing the provider online. Providers need to develop a social media monitoring program immediately to respond in the real world to issues flagged in cyberspace. Social media has become a vital tool for marketing, patient communication, and care management, and healthcare providers can become active participants[19] while staying on the right side of the law.

Table 12-2 provides keys to success.

Table 12-2. Planning For Success in Healthcare Social Media

- Inventory current goals, strategies, tactics and current policies
- Establish future goals, design strategies and tactics to support them
- Review inward-facing and outward-facing policies and procedures
- Create/update policies through an inclusive process (with legal/regulatory at the table)
- Train staff
- Kick off
- Monitor success of strategies and tactics, and adherence to policies
- Rinse (make necessary changes) and repeat

REFERENCES

1. Fox S. The social life of health information. *Pew Internet & American Life Project*. 2011. http://pewinternet.org/Reports/2011/Social-Life-of-Health-Info.aspx. Accessed December 4, 2013.

2. *e-patients.net*. Blog of The Society for Participatory Medicine. http://e-patients.net. Accessed December 4, 2013.

3. *Health Care Social Media List*. Mayo Clinic Center for Social Media. http://network.socialmedia.mayoclinic.org/hcsml-grid/. Accessed December 4, 2013.

4. Harlow D. Posts categorized "Health Reform." *HealthBlawg*. 2013. http://healthblawg.com/health-reform/. Accessed December 4, 2013.

5. Harlow D. Meaningful use: the final rule. *HealthBlawg*. 2010. http://healthblawg.com/2010/07/meaningful-use-the-final-rule.html. Accessed December 4, 2013.

6. Harlow D. Posts categorized "Accountable Care Organization." *HealthBlawg*. 2013. http://healthblawg.com/accountable-care-organization/. Accessed December 4, 2013.

7. Harlow D. Federales finalize Accountable Care Organization regs, define "patient engagement" and "patient-centeredness." *e-patients.net*. 2011. http://e-patients.net/archives/2011/10/federales-finalize-accountable-care-organization-regs-define-patient-engagement-and-patient-centeredness.html. Accessed December 4, 2013.

8. Harlow D. Posts categorized "HIPAA." *HealthBlawg*. 2013. http://www.healthblawg.com/hipaa/. Accessed December 4, 2013.

9. Harlow D. David Harlow quoted in AMA American Medical News story on daily deal websites. HealthBlawg. 2011. http://healthblawg.com/2011/03/david-harlow-quoted-in-ama-american-medical-news-story-on-daily-deal-websites.html. Accessed December 4, 2013.

10. FTC publishes final guides governing endorsements, testimonials [press release]. Washington, DC; Federal Trade Commission: October 5, 2009. http://www.ftc.gov/opa/2009/10/endortest.shtm. Accessed December 4, 2013.

11. Acting General Counsel releases report on social media cases [press release]. Washington, DC: National Labor Relations Board. August 19, 2011. http://www.nlrb.gov/news-outreach/news-story/acting-general-counsel-releases-report-social-media-cases. Accessed December 4, 2013.

12. Harlow D. Facebook misstep costs RI physician fine, job. *HealthBlawg*. 2011. http://healthblawg.com/2011/04/health-care-social-media-policies-facebook-misstep-costs-ri-physician-fine-job.html. Accessed December 4, 2013.

13. U.S. Department of Health & Human Services. *Health Information Privacy.* http://www.hhs. gov/ocr/privacy/. Accessed December 4, 2013.

14. Straw J. Woman out of a job after sending tweet to Governor Barbour. *MS News Now.* 2012. http://www.wlbt.com/story/11713360/woman-out-of-a-job-after-sending-tweet-to-governor-barbour. Accessed December 4, 2013.

15. American Medical Association Policy. *Opinion 9.124 - Professionalism in the Use of Social Media.*2011. http://www.ama-assn.org/ama/pub/physician-resources/medical-ethics/code-medical-ethics/opinion9124.page. Accessed December 4, 2013.

16. VA publishes social media policy [press release]. Washington, DC: U.S. Department of Veterans Affairs; August 16, 2011. http://www.va.gov/opa/pressrel/pressrelease. cfm?id=2150. Accessed December 4, 2013.

17. National Labor Relations Board. *The NLRB and Social Media.* http://www.nlrb.gov/node/5078. Accessed December 4, 2013.

18. Harlow D. Employee social media policies after NLRB appointments invalidated by federal court…everything you know is wrong? *HealthBlawg.* 2013. http://www.healthblawg. com/2013/02/employee-social-media-policies-after-nlrb-appointments-invalidated-by-federal-court-everything-you-k.html. Accessed December 4, 2013.

19. Harlow D. Health care social media consulting services. *HealthBlawg.* 2013. http:// healthblawg.com/health-care-social-media-consulting-services.html. Accessed December 4, 2013.

Chapter 13:

Public Engagement: Health Information Technology, Social Media, and Government Policy

Brian Ahier; Christina Beach Thielst, FACHE

In general, the United States government has been steadily embracing the use of social media. On January 21, 2009, his first full day in office, President Obama issued a Memorandum on Transparency and Open Government[1] and called for recommendations to make the federal government more transparent, participatory, and collaborative. This was followed on December 8, 2009, by the Open Government Directive,[2] which instructed every federal agency to open its doors and data to the American people. Many federal agencies struggled with implementing this new policy. This was a major cultural shift, and trying to bring such broad changes to government bureaucracy presented many challenges.

Although the use of social media is not the only aspect of this drive toward what has been termed "Government 2.0," it is one component of the attempt at greater transparency and engagement with the citizenry. As Tim O'Reilly said when introducing the concept of government as a platform, "Participation means true engagement with citizens in the business of government, and actual collaboration with citizens in the design of government programs."[3] Many federal agencies have struggled with making good use of social media tools, but the Department of Health and Human Services (HHS) has served as an example of how government can use these various platforms to improve services and engagement with the American people.

MAKING PUBLIC HEALTH INFORMATION AVAILABLE

Furthering the goals of a more digital government, the White House released the Digital Government Strategy,[4] a roadmap for building a 21st century digital government that delivers better digital services to the American people. HHS followed with the launch of the HHS Digital Strategy website[5] to showcase a vision for the future whose goal is to provide public health information whenever and wherever it is needed. Examples include:

- Making cancer information available on smartphones[6]

- Creating application programming interfaces that let people learn about influences on health in their communities[7]

- Creating one-stop shopping for critical information that opens content to persons with disabilities[8]

Building websites that deliver information where it is needed is at the center of HHS's mobile strategy. HHS agencies have responded to the increasing number of visitors to their sites who use tablets and smartphones by developing at least 33 mobile health applications (http://www.hhs.gov/digitalstrategy/mobile/mobile-apps.html) that are available for free to the public. The apps cover a range of capabilities, including tracking health status, accessing medical information, helping teens quit smoking, finding an HIV/AIDS treatment professional, tracking influenza-like illness activity, accessing a directory of health hotlines across the nation, finding community health centers, and recording current and past medication histories.

The Centers for Medicare & Medicaid Services embraced functionality used in the banking and credit industries to create a mobile app that facilitates greater transparency and accuracy in financial interactions between doctors and the healthcare industry. The Open Payments Apps allow users to track data necessary for successful program reporting required by the Open Payments Program (http://www.cms.gov/Regulations-and-Guidance/Legislation/National-Physician-Payment-Transparency-Program/index.html) of the Affordable Care Act. The apps help physicians ensure that information reported by industry about them is accurate, with real-time tracking of payments and other transfers of value received from their affiliations.

One powerful example of how social media can make timely information widely available was shown during the swine flu emergency. Efforts to distribute accurate information about the dangers of swine flu and the importance of vaccination were hampered by the sheer complexity of the message. Social media tools from HHS (http://www.hhs.gov/web/socialmedia/), the Centers for Disease and Control and Prevention (CDC) (http://www.hhs.gov/web/socialmedia/), and others were effectively used to assist in quickly disseminating information and dispelling rumors or falsehoods that had been published through unofficial sources. The government harnessed the power of Twitter, Facebook, YouTube, and blogs to reach a new audience and provide real-time information. Widgets, mobile information, online videos, and other tools reinforced and personalized messages; reached new audiences; and built a communication infrastructure based on open information exchange. Social media proved to be a powerful new method of health communication.

COLLABORATION AND CROWDSOURCING

The Office of the National Coordinator for Health Information Technology (ONC) has taken use of social media to the next level in terms of stakeholder engagement and crowdsourcing ideas as well as providing information on agency activities and promoting greater transparency. Their efforts began by using a wiki (http://wiki.directproject.org/ONC+Website) to aid in collaboration with experts across the country and shape the Direct Project. They also solicited contributions and ideas on a range of issues as well as shaped policy and strategy around some of this stakeholder input by actively listening on various platforms such as Twitter, Facebook, LinkedIn®, and Google+. From the National Coordinator to Directors to front-line staff, the ONC has discussed important issues involving standards, policies, and strategies to increase adoption of health information technology (IT) and use it more efficiently.

The ONC hosts the Health IT Buzz Blog (http://www.healthit.gov/buzz-blog/) on healthit.gov, with regular updates from various staff at all levels. Very interesting conversations have taken place via blog posts on the official ONC accounts of Twitter and Google+ as well as on personal accounts of staffers. The ONC may be one of the most advanced users of social media tools of all federal agencies. In addition to engaging with industry stakeholders and listening to the voice of the community, the ONC has adjusted policy and strategy as a result of such engagement. Social media tools have helped advance the cause of health IT and create a true community that includes clinicians, patient advocates, and policy makers.

SOCIAL SURVEILLANCE

The content on social channels offers a new pool of information to government agencies and policy makers that is more timely than traditional methods of data collection. It also offers a view of what is happening locally, regionally, or nationally that can enhance current understanding of issues and the impact of policy on communities or individuals. In addition, the information collected can confirm, enhance, and/or refute information that has been collected via more traditional methods. The benefit is more timely and comprehensive understanding of the issues and needs for more refined policy and public services.

Social surveillance, coupled with analytics, is a new technique for helping public health agencies such as the CDC track the spread of disease. Data collected from traditional techniques, including monitoring emergency department visits, gathering laboratory test results, and conducting population surveys, are now complimented with information collected from social channels.

The CDC uses social insights from predictive tools based on collective web searches and tweets on flu-related symptoms and correlates the data on regional maps. Google Flu Trends (http://www.google.org/flutrends/) uses aggregate

Google search data to provide real-time estimates of flu activity by geographic area. MappyHealth (http://mappyhealth.com/) mines real-time data from Twitter to identify health trends through the search of 234 unique terms. Mined data are displayed in graphics that assist end-users in spotting trends rapidly.

The powerful role of social media in the early identification of disease outbreaks was highlighted during the 2012/2013 flu season. The extensive flu outbreak began in late October but was not widely covered in the media until the CDC released a public warning highlighting the danger on December 3. However, in mid-October, Sickweather (http://www.sickweather.com/) sent out a tweet to users alerting them that the flu season had arrived. This data mining application scanned millions of Facebook posts and tweets for 24 flu-related symptoms, analyzed them linguistically, and plotted the data on a map.[9]

The National Library of Medicine (NLM) is proposing to mine Facebook and Twitter posts to improve its social media footprint and assess how tweets can be used as "change agents" for health behaviors. The NLM is the world's largest biomedical library, and its online information is freely available to consumers, health professionals, and biomedical scientists. This latest monitoring tool is part of their continuing quality improvement efforts to evaluate how their databases and other resources are used.[10]

The NLM believes the explosion in social media use provides a unique opportunity for sampling sentiment and use patterns of their "customers" and for comparing NLM with other sources of health-related information. They plan to examine relevant tweets and comments related to extent of use, context in which information was sought, and effects of various health-related announcements and events on usage patterns. Specifically, NLM will evaluate the "value of tweets and other messages as teaching tools and change-agents for health-relevant behavior." The overarching objective of these studies is to obtain a richer understanding of how consumers, clinicians, and researchers actually look for health-related information and what they do with what they find.[11]

INDIVIDUAL CONNECTIONS

According to a Pew Internet survey, 66% of social media users have employed the platforms to post their thoughts about civic and political issues, react to others' postings, press friends to act on issues and vote, follow candidates, "like" and link to others' content, and join groups formed on social networking sites.[12] Not surprisingly, younger individuals are more likely to use social media for civic activities.

Social media channels present additional communication routes to help professionals directly connect with key legislators and policymakers, following them in real time and sharing insights and feedback. The channels also offer politicians and policymakers an avenue of direct and unfiltered feedback from constituents in manageable doses. By using social channels, healthcare providers may connect with key individuals and help shape a more relevant strategy and policy that will have significant impact on their profession, organization, or community.

REFERENCES

1. Obama B. *Memorandum for the Heads of Executive Departments and Agencies: Subject: Transparency and Open Government*. Washington, DC: The White House; 2009. http://www.whitehouse.gov/the_press_office/Transparency_and_Open_Government/. Accessed December 4, 2013.

2. Orszag P. *Memorandum for the Heads of Executive Departments and Agencies: Subject: Open Government Directive*. Washington, DC: Executive Office of the President; 2009. http://www.whitehouse.gov/sites/default/files/omb/assets/memoranda_2010/m10-06.pdf. Accessed December 4, 2013.

3. Lathrop D, Ruma L, eds. *Open Government; Collaboration, Transparency, and Participation in Practice*. Sebastopol, CA: O'Reilly Media; 2010.

4. *Digital Government: Building a 21st Century Platform to Better Serve the American People*. Washington, DC: The White House; 2013. http://www.whitehouse.gov/sites/default/files/omb/egov/digital-government/digital-government-strategy.pdf. Accessed December 4, 2013.

5. U.S. Department of Health and Human Services. Digital strategy. *HHS.gov*. http://www.hhs.gov/digitalstrategy/. Accessed December 4, 2013.

6. U.S. Department of Health and Human Services. Create a cancer survivor tool challenge winner. *HHS.gov*. http://www.hhs.gov/digitalstrategy/mobile/cancer-survivor-tool-challenge-winner.html. Accessed December 2013.

7. U.S. Department of Health and Human Services. Data.CDC.gov: energizing data to better tell the story. *HHS.gov*. http://www.hhs.gov/digitalstrategy/open-data/data.cdc.html. Accessed December 4, 2013.

8. U.S. Department of Health and Human Services. Serving people with disability. *HHS.gov*. http://www.hhs.gov/digitalstrategy/working-better/serving-people-with-disabilities.html. Accessed December 4, 2013.

9. Konkel F. Predictive analytics allows feds to track outbreaks in real time. *FCW*. 2013. http://fcw.com/articles/2013/01/25/flu-social-media.aspx. Accessed December 4, 2013.

10. National Institutes of Health. Social media and engagement tool software: evaluating on-line resources of the national library of medicine by mining social media. *FedBizOpps.gov*. https://www.fbo.gov/index?s=opportunity&mode=form&id=63cad44a4b0de5087204f9b142ae8231. Accessed December 4, 2013.

11. National Institutes of Health. Response to inquiries: request for quote (RFQ) NIHLM2013659SRE: social media and engagement tool. FedBizOpps.gov. https://www.fbo.gov/utils/view?id=8f17eabe380cfecc59b532ebec90efe4. Accessed December 4, 2013.

12. Rainie L, Smith A, Schlozman KL, Brady H. Verba S. Social media and political engagement. Pew Internet & American Life Project. 2012. http://pewinternet.org/Reports/2012/Political-engagement.aspx. Accessed December 4, 2013.

Glossary

Brad Tritle, CIPP

Aggregator: An application or website that collects specified syndicated, web-based news feeds (see also RSS).

App: 1) A software application used on a mobile device (e.g., mobile phone, tablet); 2) A "mini" software application, such as a widget, used to enable a specific functionality on a web or social media platform (see also Widget).

Avatar: An image or figure, frequently movable or animated, representing a user while participating in a virtual world, or in place of a user photo on a social networking profile.

Blog*: Short for "web log," used to refer to sites maintained by one person (most commonly) or one organization/company for the purpose of sharing thoughts describing the author's life or focused on a particular topic or suite of topics.

Blogger: An author of a blog.

Blogroll: A list of an individual's or organization's recommended or frequently read blogs.

Branding: Creating an image or name that differentiates an individual or organization as part of a marketing strategy. Astute organizations use social media to enhance an existing brand or build a new brand, but mismanagement of social media (e.g., inappropriate responses to customer/patient comments) by organizations can detract from a brand's perception.

Buttons: See Social Sharing Buttons.

Collaborative Projects*: Social media sites dedicated to facilitating collaboration around a chosen topic or project. These include wikis (primarily text-based) and social bookmark sites (see definitions of both).

Content Marketing: Developing and sharing content on websites and social media for the purpose of increasing engagement with existing or potential customers, ultimately with the goal of increasing loyalty and/or sales.

Crowd Sourcing*: Using social media to request input on problems or questions that traditionally would be addressed within an organization. The request for input may be to the public or an individual may seek input specifically from those with whom he or she is connected on a social media platform.

Crowd Funding: Building on the concept of crowd sourcing, this approach expands from sourcing of ideas and solutions to raising funds through online contributions of many. This concept is helping people build businesses as well as individuals, groups, and hospitals to fundraise. It is a component of "ephilanthropy," which used by nonprofits to build relationships, raise funds, and organize constituents online.

Editorial Schedule (see Publication Schedule)**:** A calendar of planned social media posts and/or activities, such as blog posts and topic-based discussions.

Enterprise Social Media*: The use of social media technologies in a closed, secure, and private environment, such as behind a corporate firewall.

Geo-location*: A geographic location associated with a social media user's activity. A geo-location could be a latitude/longitude, country, city, or as specific as a retail store or healthcare facility such as a practice or hospital (see also Geotagging).

Geotagging: The act of associating or tagging a social media post, which may include a photo or video with its geo-location.

Handle: A nickname on a social medial platform that is associated with an individual or organizational account.

Hashtag (#): Both a noun and verb. Noun – a standardized tag to associate a social media post with a category or subject, including time-limited/scheduled or ongoing social media discussions related to the subject. The named category is immediately preceded by the pound/hashtag sign (#). Examples include: #HITsm (Health IT social media), #patientengagement, and #EHR. Verb – to tag a phrase or subject using the pound/hashtag sign (#).

Infographic: A graphic image, or compilation of images, designed to engage the viewer and enhance the speed of data and information comprehension. By replacing text with an image, an infographic facilitates large amounts of information being easily understood and shared via social media.

Live Chat: 1) A scheduled, time-limited, synchronous (real-time), and often topic-driven discussion using social media. 2) Live chat may also refer to the real-time, unscheduled or scheduled, online engagement of users of a website or social media site, either with each other or with a customer service representative. 3) The social technology (i.e., live chat function) that enables such discussions.

Lurking: Passively participating on social media by following others' activities without generating content oneself.

Microblog**: Real-time tools for posting comments from a computer or handheld device. Usually a character-limited blog post that can include status updates as part of a multifunctional social media platform as well as sites that are dedicated to frequent sharing of real-time, character-limited content to followers.

Moderator: An individual who hosts and manages an online discussion (e.g., live chat) or meeting. This person's responsibilities may include welcoming participants, ensuring the chat stays on topic, moving through scheduled topics according to an agenda, and closing out the discussion by thanking participants. A moderated chat or discussion is one hosted by a moderator.

Online Forum: A site specifically for the purpose of hosting online/web-based discussions. It facilitates asynchronous (non-real-time) participation and is often used either for public discussion on a specific topic or by an organization to facilitate discussions on various topics of interest to the organization's members.

Patient Engagement Index: A scale-based rating for an organization derived from an algorithmically based calculation of multiple inputs, such as social media engagement, patient satisfaction survey scores, and availability of self-management tools.

Plug-in: A downloadable software script that can be used by a website designer or user to enhance the functionality of a site (e.g., blog or search engine home page). A Widget is often derived from a Plug-in (see Widget).

Podcast: An audio-only or multimedia recording available as a download from a website or purchasable (free or paid) through an app store. A podcast may be available as a one-time download or as an ongoing subscription to regularly scheduled recordings. Podcasts are similar to and may also be recordings of radio-based talk shows, news shows, and interviews.

Privacy Settings: A section of a social media site or affiliated functionality that allows the user to adjust the visibility of his or her personal information (e.g., birthday, geographic location), activity (e.g., posts), or the ease with which others may communicate with the user.

Publication Schedule (also Editorial Schedule)**:** A calendar of planned social media posts and activities, such as blog posts and discussions.

Return on Investment (ROI)*: A calculation showing an organization's or individual's net results (financial or otherwise) from participation in social media. Strictly speaking, the calculation is derived from dividing the new results or new revenue attributed to social media activity by the amount of money invested or spent to achieve the results or revenue ([New Revenue − Investment]/Investment). Some organizations may also calculate ROI based on benefits generated from increased brand recognition or perception, customer loyalty, or customer satisfaction.

RSS*: An abbreviation for "Really Simple Syndication." RSS feeds send updates from online resources, such as blogs, wikis, and websites, to desktops and mobile devices. RSS feeds may be accumulated and read within Microsoft® Outlook, any number of standalone RSS (news) reader applications, or an RSS-enabled Internet browser.

Search Engine: A searchable index of webpages that is updated through the crawling (searching and indexing by words and keywords) of websites. The index often includes a ranking of pages based on relevance, frequency of updates, number of other pages referencing/linking to them, geographic proximity (e.g., restaurant, doctor's office, hospital) to the user (based on IP address), or other factors.

Search Engine Optimization (SEO): The process of affecting the visibility of a website in a search engine's unpaid results, often used as a marketing strategy known as Search Engine Marketing (SEM). Tactics may include increasing the presence of frequently searched keywords in the website's content or coding (e.g., HTML) or promoting the site online so that other sites link to it.

Social Bookmarking: A site that allows users to save, import, annotate, and share web-based links.

Social Intelligence: The use of social media platforms to perform intelligence-gathering activities.

Social Media: Online or mobile environments created for the purpose of social interaction or collaboration.

Social Media Hub, or Social Hub: 1) A location on a corporate or individual's website or blog where content from the user's (individual's or corporation's) social media accounts is aggregated. 2) A single social media application used to interface with a user's other social media applications.

Social Media Tabs: Functionality enabled by and contained within a widget that allows a website user to scroll through the site's associated social media accounts.

Social Networking Sites: Originally sites where users built an online profile and connected that profile with others to build a network, the sites now offer a variety of activities among members of the networks. Such activities may include posting of microblogs or status updates, instant messaging, videoconferencing, and sharing bookmarks. Many social media sites have social networking as an underlying function or enabler.

Social Media Policy*: An organization's code of conduct for employees regarding their social media activity as well as the conduct of others (e.g., patients, the public) who may interact with the organization's social media accounts. The policy may include value statements, privacy policies, best practices, and limitations.

Social Sharing Buttons: Small images on a webpage that facilitate sharing of that page's content via social media. Clicking on a button frequently auto-generates a link and/or post and an interface for the viewer/user to enter his or her username and password for that social media platform, authorizing the content sharing/post on his or her behalf.

Social Surveillance: The use of social media to ascertain the activities of others, ranging from individuals observing their friends, family, or acquaintances to the use of social media for public health surveillance purposes.

Social Technologies: Technologies/functionalities that enable online or mobile interaction or collaboration. Examples include blogs, microblogs, wikis, web conferencing, and social networking. A social media site or platform can build its business and operations using one or more social technologies.

Virtual World: An online community, often three-dimensional, where users are represented by icons or figures, usually movable, known as avatars. In a virtual world, users may interact with others, learn, teach, participate in conferences, use or build objects, and even participate in a virtual economy.

Vlog: A video blog.

Widget**: Chunks of code or mini-applications that perform a specific function and enhance the content of the site. Widgets can conduct short surveys, present slide shows, or map activities or conditions on websites, blogs, or other social media sites. Buttons and badges are graphic code that link to another site or page. A widget may also be referred to as a "plug-in."

Wiki*: A website that allows users to collaborate in a text-based fashion on a given topic (see also Collaborative Projects).

*Definition is sourced or derived from Healthcare Information and Management Systems Society (HIMSS). *Healthcare "Friending" Social Media: What Is It, How Is It Used, And What Should I Do?* December 2, 2012. www.himss.org/asp/contentredirector.asp?contentid=79496. Accessed August 3, 2013.

**Definition is sourced or derived from Thielst CB. *Social Media in Healthcare: Connect, Communicate, Collaborate.* 2nd ed. Chicago, IL: Health Administration Press; 2013.

Index